LIVING LIKE JESUS

Also by Ronald J. Sider

Cup of Water, Bread of Life
Good News and Good Works
Rich Christians in an Age of Hunger
Christ and Violence
Completely Pro-Life

LIVING LIKE JESUS

Eleven Essentials
for Growing a Genuine Faith

Ronald J. Sider

Baker Books

A Division of Baker Book House Co
Grand Rapids, Michigan 49516

To Arbutus

CONTENTS

ACKNOWLEDGMENTS

Heidi Rolland, my graduate assistant, brought her outstanding gifts and wonderful dedication to the double task of research and proofreading. Robertoluis Lugo, the faculty secretary who carefully typed and retyped this manuscript, is actually beginning to believe my claim that there is a discernible pattern in the obscure scrawl that I call handwriting. With her normal blend of skill and kindness, Naomi Miller, my administrative secretary, helped keep the rest of my activities on track while I wrote.

Thanks to all my special partners at Baker, especially Dwight Baker and Robert Hosack, for the second edition of this book.

To my parents, James and Ida Sider, I say thanks for the way they modeled genuine Christianity without guile or hypocrisy. The joyful integrity and goodness of their example decade after decade nurtured in their children a powerful desire to live like Christ. For all that they taught me, I will be eternally grateful.

Most of all, I thank my wife, Arbutus—to whom I dedicate this book. She is God's best gift to me after his Son. Her steadfast desire to love and obey Christ above everything else and then to walk with me in faithful covenant through struggle, ecstasy, and deepening joy has provided the most important human support for my journey toward genuine Christianity. For her gentle, faithful love over thirty-seven years of growth in mutual submission, joy, and intimacy, I thank her with all my heart.

9

CHARACTERISTICS
OF A GENUINE CHRISTIAN

1. Genuine Christians embrace both God's holiness and God's love
2. Genuine Christians live like Jesus
3. Genuine Christians keep their marriage covenants and put children before career
4. Genuine Christians nurture daily spiritual renewal and live in the power of the Spirit
5. Genuine Christians strive to make the church a little picture of what heaven will be like
6. Genuine Christians love the whole person the way Jesus did
7. Genuine Christians mourn church divisions and embrace all who confess Jesus as God and Savior
8. Genuine Christians confess that Jesus is Lord of politics and economics
9. Genuine Christians share God's special concern for the poor
10. Genuine Christians treasure the creation and worship the creator
11. Genuine Christians embrace servanthood

INTRODUCTION

What would it take to change this world–to really change it for the better?

I think the answer is simple: It would take just a tiny fraction of today's Christians truly believing what Jesus taught and living the way Jesus lived.

Imagine for a moment this astonishing, imaginary conversation that Jesus might have had with the archangel Gabriel upon his triumphant return to heaven.

"Well, how did it go?" Gabriel asks Jesus. "Did you complete your mission and save the world?"

"Well, yes and no," Jesus replies. "I modeled a godly life for about thirty years. I preached to a few thousand Jews in one corner of the Roman Empire. I died for the sins of the world and promised that those who believe in me will live forever. And I burst from the tomb on the third day to show my circle of 120 frightened followers that my life and story are God's way to save the whole world. Then I gave the Holy Spirit to those 120 and left them to finish the task."

"You mean," Gabriel asks in amazement, "your whole plan to save the world depends on that ragtag bunch of fishermen, ex-prostitutes, and tax collectors?"

"That's right," Jesus replies.

"But what if they fail?" Gabriel persists with growing alarm. "What's your backup plan?"

"There is no backup plan," Jesus says quietly.

And there is still no backup plan. God has decided to use human beings, not angels, to spread the gospel and change the world.

Gabriel watched dumbfounded as that motley crew set to work—with little money, less education, and no political clout. But because they loved Jesus with all their hearts and knew he was the way, the truth, and the life for all people everywhere, they defied raging oceans and roaring lions to preach and live Jesus' Good News, and the message spread like wildfire. Within three centuries, that growing circle had conquered the most powerful pagan empire that ever existed.

As the centuries rolled by, Gabriel marveled as Christianity spread west to Europe, south to Africa, north to Russia, then farther west to the Americas. Finally, in the explosive missionary fervor of the nineteenth and twentieth centuries, he saw the Christian faith sweep across Africa and multiply rapidly in many parts of Asia. The 120 people in the upper room had become almost two billion living in every country on the planet.

Far more people have come to Christ in this century than in any previous one. Mission specialist David Barrett estimates that today the number of committed Christians (whom he calls "Great Commission" Christians) is growing more than twice as fast as the total world population.[1]

Christianity has become the first truly global religion. In 1900, about 75 percent of all Christians were white people living in Europe, Russia, and North America. By 2000, 56 percent of all Christians will live in the Third World. Believers in Africa, Asia, and Latin America have increased 1,300 percent in a hundred years and will number about 1.2 billion by the year 2000.

Without a backup plan, Jesus' strategy was working, and now as Gabriel peers into the future at the end of the twentieth century, he sees many reasons for hope. The global context is more favorable, in many ways, than it was even fifty years ago. For a major part of the twentieth century, almost half of the world's people lived under oppressive governments, with Marxism as one of the most serious threats to Christianity. But atheistic communism has collapsed, and today most nations embrace the democratic ideal–at least with their lips. Freedom to spread the gospel and live as Christians has vastly expanded.

Paralyzing poverty has also been substantially reduced. In earlier times, most people lived at the subsistence level. In this century, however, new technologies and market systems have created enormous new wealth. Malnutrition has decreased significantly in the last twenty years.[2]

The twenty-first century could be Christianity's finest hour.[3]

As Gabriel ponders more carefully, however, an old anxiety resurfaces. In the centuries since Jesus returned to heaven, vast numbers claimed to be Christians without living what Jesus taught. Were the people who claimed the name notably different from those who did not?

How could the worst massacre of Jews in human history have happened in the middle of Europe–the continent that had been "Christian" for the longest time? How could some of the most vicious tribal slaughter occur in Rwanda, where 80 percent of the people, both Hutus and Tutsis, were Christians? How could Catholic Christian Croatians and Orthodox Christian Serbs massacre each other and Muslims in one of the most deadly outbreaks of ethnic savagery in Europe since Hitler?

And what about the United States? It is rich, powerful, and more "Christian" than almost any other nation on earth–86 percent of its people claim to be Christians, and almost 50 percent go to church every Sunday.

But does Christianity make any difference in their personal lives? With the highest divorce rate in human history, today's "Christians" are doing to their children what no other generation or civilization has ever done.

Relativism has invaded Christian minds. Sixty-two percent of so-called "born again" Christians do *not* believe in absolute truth.[4] The murder rate in the United States is almost twice that of the industrialized country with the second highest murder rate. The United States jails a higher percentage of its population than any other nation.[5] Violence and drugs stalk its inner cities. "Christians" are highly visible in politics, but Jesus' passion for the poor rarely surfaces on their agenda. Collapsing values, growing uncertainty, and wrenching brokenness plague the churches.

Is Jesus' strategy for changing the world really working? The picture isn't entirely clear to Gabriel. Vast numbers of so-called Christians live just like their secular neighbors.

Here and there, however, small groups like the original 120 seem to be making Jesus the central passion in their lives. Gabriel thinks of Wayne Gordon, a pastor in one of the poorest, most violent sections of inner-city Chicago. Soon after his conversion as a teenager, Gordon looked into the face of God and promised, "I will do anything that you want me to do with my life." He therefore defied roaches, break-ins, and violence to tell inner-city kids–with virtually no hope of a decent education, job, or marriage–that the Creator of the universe loves them and wants them to live with him eternally. Because Wayne followed Jesus' example of caring for the whole person, he also started tutoring programs, recreational services, a health clinic, a job training facility, low-income housing, and small businesses. After twenty years, God has blessed Wayne's faith, prayer, and hard work with a thriving, interracial church of five hundred people and a vast, holistic multimillion-dollar community center that is transforming one of the most devastated sections of Chicago.[6]

Gabriel sees other committed Christians–thousands and thousands of them–scattered all around the world who live joyfully with Jesus as the center of their lives. Everywhere they are leading people to Christ, throwing their arms around the needy, and walking arm-in-arm with these broken people as Christ restores them to wholeness. Their ministries renew broken families, empower the poor, and transform violent neighborhoods. They correct environmental pollution and work for freedom, peace, life, and social justice. Again and again, their labor, goodness, and integrity slowly improve whole communities and entire nations.

Yes, Gabriel concludes, *Jesus' strategy does work–when the people who claim the name of Christ are unconditionally committed to him.*

Even a small percent of today's 1.9 billion Christians could easily change the world in dramatic ways;[7] the ravages of divorce could be reversed; almost everyone could enjoy a decent job and adequate income; violence, racism, and war could recede–if only a fraction of Jesus' followers practice what he preached.

As Gabriel peers into the third millennium of Jesus' astonishing game plan, he asks himself: *Will there be enough Christians like the original 120?*

Slowly, a wondrous dream floods his mind. He dreams of tens of millions of genuine followers of Jesus moving boldly into every city, town, and village on planet earth. They model joyous marriages and wholesome family life. They love the earth, care for creation, and develop sustainable technologies that produce wealth and wholeness for themselves and their great-grandchildren. They measure their societies by whether they strengthen the weak and care for the poor. They gladly tell everyone who will listen that the center of their joy is Jesus the Savior, and they welcome an ever-growing number from every tribe and nation into the new community of disciples.

To be sure, Gabriel foresees, there will still be many non-Christians. Even most of those who claim Jesus' name will still look a lot more like the world than like Jesus. Brokenness, injustice, fear, and war will not disappear entirely. Jesus will have to complete his victory later when he chooses to return to the little planet he had visited once in the days of Caesar Augustus.

But for now—in Gabriel's dream—Jesus' plan is working. Deeply committed Christians are a minority, to be sure, but there are enough disciples who dare—like Wayne and that first 120—to look into the face of Christ and vow: "If you give me the power, I'll do whatever you want me to." And the world is changing.

You and I will face breathtaking possibilities and deadly dangers in the next millennium. It could be hell. Or it could be Christianity's finest hour.

Jesus' goal and his strategy will continue to be the same. He will continue to plead with you and me to surrender every fiber of our being to him and to carry his salvation to the ends of the earth because he longs for everyone to know his salvation. As Creator, he also wants everyone to enjoy an abundant life on this good little planet.

It's up to us.

There is no backup plan.

1

SEARING HOLINESS, FORGIVING LOVE

Characteristic One

Genuine Christians embrace both God's holiness and God's love

For thirty-seven years, my wife and I have lived together in what Richard Foster rightly calls "a mixture of ecstasy and halitosis." Mostly it has been joy. But there have been times of struggle as well.

The most painful time for Arbutus and me came in our late thirties. No, we did not commit adultery, but we caused each other great pain. I confess, sadly, that my anger would sometimes blaze so furiously that I wanted to hurt her deeply. Partly to wound her and partly to satisfy my sinful desires, I probably would have had an adulterous affair, but for one thing–I knew it was sin. A holy God hates adultery. I knew I could not break my marriage vow and still look eagerly into the loving eyes of my Lord. His righteous commands protected me when my own strength was weak. The biblical truth about God's holiness guarded my step and kept me from inflicting pain on the person I loved more than anyone in the world.

That is not to pretend that I did not sin against Arbutus. Our marriage was in crisis, and there were days when I wondered if it would even survive. But it was precisely during those days I gained a deeper understanding of the cross. As I pondered the wounds that Arbutus and I had inflicted on each other, I realized we had three choices. We could pretend that our sin was not important, that it didn't matter–which would have been a lie. Or we could have shouted: "That's it. I'll never forgive you–" which would have ended our relationship. Both options would have made reconciliation impossible.

There was another possibility, however. I had to say to Arbutus–and she to me–"Your betrayal was awful. It hurt terribly. But I love you. I love you so much that I will take the evil you have done into my heart and forgive you. I can't say it was nothing. But I don't want to live forever estranged and hostile. So I will accept the wounds of your wickedness and purify them with my love and forgiveness."

That's what God did on the cross. Our sins are too awful for God to wink at, yet his love is too strong for God to forget us. So God embraces our sin, absorbs our evil into his divine heart, and accepts the punishment we deserve–all because God wants to walk with us again in openness and reconciliation.

The cross is the only satisfactory solution to the brokenness, violence, and agony of our world. It is the most amazing solution to the problem of evil the world has ever known, for no other religion dares to teach that the Creator of the universe died for our sins.

The cross, however, only makes sense if we understand that God is a righteous Sovereign as well as a loving Father. If anything is clear in Scripture, it is that blazing holiness is just as central to God's character as overflowing mercy. Jesus taught clearly that the awesome Creator of the galaxies is indeed a tender, loving Father. But at the same time, Jesus repeatedly warned that sinners will be separated eternally from this holy Judge.

The modern church wants to accept only half of God. It seeks to renegotiate God's revelation. It substitutes a new covenant and a new God who offers forgiveness without holiness.

The biblical God beckons us to return and rediscover who God really is. God summons us to bow in awe before his searing holiness as we praise God for his astounding love. Only then will the church truly understand God, sin, and salvation. Only then will it recover its strength.

The modern church wants a cosmic Santa Claus who produces wealth, health, and happiness to bolster our good feelings and self-esteem. We prefer a divine Buddy who smiles kindly at sin with an "Aw shucks, pal, we all mess up sometimes."

The modern church wants to forget sin. We prefer to write our own guidelines for happiness.

The modern church wants to neglect repentance and sanctification. We prefer to replace holiness with happiness.

Is it really any wonder that so many contemporary Christians and churches are disastrously weak and disgracefully ineffective?

Isaiah and Jesus knew that God combines holiness and love in a marvelous, astonishing way.

When Isaiah encountered the living God in the temple, he was overwhelmed by God's majesty and his own sin.

> I saw the Lord seated on a throne, high and exalted, and the train of his robe filled the temple. Above him were seraphs. . . . And they were calling to one another:
>
> "Holy, holy, holy is the LORD Almighty;
> the whole earth is full of his glory."
>
> At the sound of their voices the doorposts and thresholds shook and the temple was filled with smoke. "Woe to me!" I cried. "I am ruined! For I am a man of unclean lips, . . . and my eyes have seen the King, the LORD Almighty."

Isaiah 6:1–5

Isaiah knew that he and his people had disobeyed many of God's commandments. They often worshiped idols and regularly neglected the poor, the widow, and the orphan. Perhaps he remembered the divine warning: "Do not take advantage of a widow or an orphan. If you do . . . my anger will be aroused, and I will kill you with the sword" (Exod. 22:22–24).

Nor is God's wrath just a passing peculiarity of the Old Testament. The apostle of grace and freedom never hesitated to underline God's holy hatred of sin: "For the wrath of God is revealed from heaven against all ungodliness and wickedness of those who by their wickedness suppress the truth" (Rom. 1:18 NRSV; see also Eph. 5:5–6). Jesus himself warned that those who do not obey his command to feed the hungry will hear the terrifying words: "Depart from me, you who are cursed, into the eternal fire prepared for the devil and his angels" (Matt. 25:41).

Thank God that this is only half of what the Bible tells us about him. As Isaiah repented, God quickly dispatched an angelic messenger to assure him that his sins were forgiven, so that Isaiah could then compare God to a mother eagle who gently swoops down to save a falling eaglet still learning to fly (Deut. 32:11–12). To further portray the extent of God's incredible longing to draw us back to the divine embrace, Isaiah also describes God as a mother lov-

20

ingly suffering the anguish of childbirth: "Like a woman in childbirth, I cry out, I gasp and pant," God says (Isa. 42:14; also 49:15). God promises to comfort us "as a mother comforts her child" (Isa. 66:13).

Jesus compared God to the father of the prodigal son, eagerly, expectantly, waiting to forgive wandering sons and daughters who repent. At the cross, in the second person of the Trinity, the majestic Creator and holy Judge suffered the agony of Roman crucifixion because in his overflowing love God does not want anyone to perish (2 Peter 3:9).

To astonished contemporaries who saw God primarily as a distant Sovereign and righteous Judge, Jesus taught that God is also Father. In fact, among his many departures from tradition, he insisted that we can even use the tender word "Daddy" when we address the Creator of the galaxies. No matter what our sin, no matter how outrageous our rebellion, God stands ready to welcome us into his forgiving, fatherly embrace.

Righteousness and holiness on the one hand, love and forgiveness on the other—only when we grasp the full biblical teaching about both aspects of God can we genuinely understand sin and salvation.

Tragically, modern people dislike the idea of sin. This is really quite odd. As the famous theologian Reinhold Niebuhr once said, original sin is perhaps the only Christian doctrine that is empirically verifiable.

Modern folk pretend otherwise. In a dozen different ways our contemporaries reject the biblical claim that all people are in disastrous rebellion against the Creator's commandments. The eighteenth-century Enlightenment rejected divine revelation as the source of what is good. Instead they placed humanity at the center of the universe and grounded ethics in autonomous humanity. Then Marx, Darwin, and Freud claimed that persons are totally determined by their environment. Since ethical ideas are merely the relativistic by-product of economic life, evolution, or our early childhood, nothing is universally right or wrong. Furthermore, the environment, not the individual, is responsible for what happens. Bertrand Russell, one of the most famous philosophers of the twentieth century illustrates the relativistic conclusion that follows: "Those who have the best poison gas will have the ethics of the future."

Current culture adds its own sad spin to this prevailing relativism. Pop psychology assures us that whatever feels good is right, that we have a right to self-fulfillment. If a spouse is not meeting your "needs," then you had better find someone else who will or it may do terrible things to your psyche.

Some misguided Christians quickly step forward to provide theological arguments to support this relativistic nonsense. Some preachers have developed a gospel of self-esteem, while ignoring the fact of sin. Others preach a gospel of personal wealth while ignoring the needs of the poor and hungry. Some radical feminists dismiss all language about God's justice and holiness as oppressive paternalism. One prominent Christian television personality shared her spiritual wisdom in a book with the heretical title *I Gotta Be Me*.[1]

While some people reject the idea of sin, others use its universality as an excuse to ignore it. How many times have you heard somebody refuse to condemn some activity that the Bible specifically calls sin with the plea: "But we're all sinners, aren't we?" But the fact that we all sin and fail to keep God's law does not mean that we should stop calling such disobedience sin. It simply means that as we condemn racism or adultery, we also cast ourselves on God's grace to ask forgiveness for our own disobedience.

In this relativistic culture, some people pretend that humans are basically good and that character flaws are simply the result of environmental conditioning. They argue that there is no universal right or wrong and, therefore, whatever feels good is right. But God disagrees. The Creator of the universe is the source of ethical truth. Rebellion against the standards God has embedded in creation and revealed in the Bible is sin and has eternal consequences.

After David raped Bathsheba and murdered her husband, he repented and pleaded with God for forgiveness. Psalm 51 rejects the modern notion that moral failure is just a subjective human affair: "Against you, you only, have I sinned and done what is evil in your sight" (v. 4). David had also sinned terribly against Bathsheba and her husband, but David knew his sin was first of all rebellion against the righteous commandments of a holy God and deserved God's punishment.

Paul insisted that sin keeps people from heaven (Gal. 5:19–21), and Jesus warned that sin condemns people to hell (Matt. 25:44–46). If Paul and Jesus knew what they were talking about, then sin is desperately important. That may not fit with modern ideas, but it corresponds to the biblical doctrine of God. Repeatedly, the New Testament teaches that those who sin are enemies of God. It is only through the cross of Christ that sinners can be saved from God's righteous wrath (Rom. 5:9–10). Only when we genuinely understand God, do we truly understand sin. Only when we understand both can we grasp the fullness of salvation.

It is hardly surprising that modern Christians who reject half of God and almost all of sin barely understand salvation. Some reduce salvation to a one-way ticket to heaven that has little effect on how they live now. Others reduce it to psychological wholeness, self-esteem, happiness, or socioeconomic well-being.

In the Bible, however, salvation is costly and holistic.

Sin is so serious that the One who created the universe had to suffer crucifixion. If we see Jesus as simply some innocent human being knocked around by an angry God we totally misunderstand the cross. The person nailed there is none other than the second person of the Trinity–

God become flesh. It is God himself who suffers unspeakable agony on Good Friday.

Why would the Creator of fifty billion galaxies come to this tiny planet to be crucified? Because sin is so awful that it cannot be ignored. And because God's astounding love is greater than God's hatred of sin. Sin is too serious to dismiss with a casual rebuke or a friendly "everybody does it." Sin distorts God's good universe. Sin violates God's holiness. Sin ravages the earth. A just, holy God rightly punishes sin.

Mercifully, however, the divine Father also eagerly yearns to draw us back to the divine embrace. Accepting the punishment our sins deserved, God offers us unmerited forgiveness for all our foolish rebellion. Furthermore, God wants to do even more than just forgive us. God also desires to change us! In fact, God longs to restore people, society, even the creation itself to the wholeness God intended.

If salvation were only forgiveness—whether received through some born-again experience or by regular participation in the sacraments—Christians would be on the way to eternal life without having to change their racist or adulterous or selfish actions. But biblical salvation is far more than just forgiveness.[2]

Consider, for example, my friends Addie and Michael Banks. Twenty years ago their marriage was on the rocks. They hated each other. The only reason they stayed together, Michael says, was to destroy each other. Then one day Addie accepted Christ. While her anger did not totally disappear, she was so obviously different that Michael also soon became a Christian. But Jesus did not produce a quick fix in their marriage. Old pain reinforced old patterns. Quarrels and fighting continued. Michael finally lost all hope that God could restore their marriage.

In despair, he said to Addie, "Why don't you go your way, and I'll go mine?"

Addie's instant response reflects a profound truth about the biblical understanding of salvation: "If God has reconciled us to himself but cannot reconcile us to each other, then the whole thing is a fraud."

Biblical salvation is for more than just reconciliation with God. It must also transform the character and lifestyle of believers. Genuine faith in Christ brings repentance, a radical turning away from sin, and a new life of holiness. God's standard, Jesus insisted, is clear: "Be perfect, therefore, as your heavenly Father is perfect" (Matt. 5:48). We never quite arrive in this life, but in the power of the Spirit we can be wondrously changed. We can overcome sinful patterns. "Those who belong to Christ Jesus have crucified the flesh with its passions and desires" (Gal. 5:24 RSV).

Paul teaches that Christ has bridged the vast gulf between a holy God and sinful people. Believers can now look directly into the holy, tender face of God and behold his glory. As we do that day by day, we "are being transformed into his likeness with ever-increasing glory" (2 Cor. 3:18). As we keep our eyes fixed on Christ, the Holy Spirit actually remakes our broken personalities, conforming us more and more to the very pattern of Jesus of Nazareth.

Nor is salvation merely an individual affair. The church is supposed to be a new, redeemed community—a little picture of what heaven will be like. Jesus Christ "gave himself for us to redeem us from all wickedness and to purify for himself a *people* that are his very own, eager to do what is good" (Titus 2:14, emphasis added). The early church broke down the sinful dividing walls that created hostility between women and men, Jews and Gentiles, slaves and masters. In Christ's new transformed community, they were truly one. And their redeemed unity and mutual love was part of the gospel Paul preached (Eph. 3:1–6).

Biblical salvation creates a new Christian community, but when Christ returns he will even restore the groaning creation to wholeness. "The creation itself will be liberated from its bondage to decay and brought into the glorious freedom of the children of God" (Rom. 8:21). Revelation even declares the breathtaking truth that when Christ returns, "the kings of the earth will bring their splendor" into the new Jerusalem (Rev. 21:24) and "the glory and honor of the nations will be brought into it" (Rev. 21:26).

If we understand salvation, we will not rest with forgiveness and neglect personal holiness. We will not be satisfied as isolated saints and overlook Christ's new redeemed community of disciples. Nor will we focus exclusively on the church and forget that God even intends to repair the ghastly distortions Satan has introduced into creation and society. The God who chose to die for us will settle for nothing less than total victory over all sin's devastation.[3]

It is a glorious paradox that the best way to happiness is not to seek it directly. Someone has rightly said that Christ "died not to make us happy, but to make us holy."[4] But holy living is not dull and burdensome. When we make personal happiness and self-fulfillment our goal, we reap the stifling boredom and evil that come from ever growing self-centeredness. But when we seek holiness rather than happiness, we get happiness too.

My wife, Arbutus, and I discovered this truth in our personal lives. As we sought to obey God in our marriage, we discovered renewed and deeper joy. An understanding of God's holy demands helped save us from some of the brokenness and hell that stalk our world. But we also discovered that failure, sin, and pain somehow manage to sneak into even the best human relationships. At that point of betrayal, the only way to reconciliation is the costly forgiveness God displayed at the cross.

Without forgiveness, marriage cannot be healed, children and parents cannot be reconciled, ethnic hostilities cannot be transcended, economic classes cannot be united. Without forgiveness, the ghastly rupture of broken relationships in home and society can only grow larger. Without forgiveness, oppression and retaliation, violence and counterviolence can only spread ever further. Without forgiveness, hell yawns ever wider and broken humanity slips slowly into the abyss.

But with forgiveness, all things—some now and some later—can be made whole. With forgiveness, and the transforming work of the Spirit, the agony of broken homes in our hurting society can be ended. With forgiveness, repentance, and redeemed lifestyles, the ghastly ethnic and racial divisions that threaten to tear today's world apart can cease. With forgiveness, and the justice that flows from Christ's compassion, the economic divisions that condemn some to deadly starvation and others to suffocating affluence can give way to wholeness for all.

I don't pretend for a minute that such perfection will happen in human history. Only when Christ returns will all things be made new. But Christians who know about the wholeness of God's salvation will begin now to live like Jesus in their personal lives, in the church, and in the world. As they do, the fruits of God's salvation spill over into society, penetrating like salt and light.

But only if we understand the God revealed in Scripture. Only if we grasp the full biblical truth about sin and salvation. If we believe only that part of God's Word that seems acceptable to today's society, we will be a sad, weak echo of the world. But if we embrace the fullness of biblical truth about God, sin, and salvation, we will be a mighty people that God will use to change our world.

Part **1**

THE INDIVIDUAL

2

CONFORMED TO CHRIST

Characteristic Two

Genuine Christians live like Jesus

Most Christians mimic the world. They are often as self-centered, as sexually promiscuous, as racist and materialistic as their unbelieving friends. They worship wealth, commit adultery, file for divorce, and destroy the environment like their neighbors.

Blatant, disobedient conformity to the world has plagued Christians for centuries. We have launched vicious crusades to slaughter Muslims, we have fabricated "biblical" arguments to justify slavery and racism, we have participated in pogroms—indeed even the Holocaust itself—against the Jews. Now, as the modern world redefines happiness as individual self-fulfillment and ever expanding material abundance, we construct new gospels of wealth and self-esteem. The world sneers at our hypocrisy, convinced that Christians, who largely defy the One they allegedly worship, have nothing to offer.

At one time, Mahatma Gandhi, the greatest Hindu of the twentieth century, seriously considered accepting the claims

31

of Christ because he loved the Jesus of the Gospels. But when he compared how Christians live with the teachings of Jesus, Gandhi turned away in revulsion. He said, "I consider Western Christianity in its practical working a negation of Christ's Christianity."[1]

Thank God that is not the whole story. Even at the worst of times, a faithful remnant has dared to challenge the status quo by living like Jesus. Corrie ten Boom risked death to defend the Jews in Holland during World War II. A century and a half earlier, William Wilberforce labored for three decades to end slavery in the British Empire. In our century, Mother Teresa tenderly cared for the poor and protected the unborn. Many Christians today joyfully keep their marriage vows in spite of Hollywood's madness.

But why are such nonconformists—the Christians who live like Jesus—so few? That is a question that drives me to tears—and even to doubt.

As a college student, I used to struggle with intellectual questions about the truth of Christianity, and while today those doubts are gone, one thing continues to cause doubt in my mind: the church. What can justify the existence of a disobedient church in which the majority of Christians live daily lives that are almost indistinguishable from those of unbelievers?

If the gospel were only the forgiveness of sins, then the scandal of Christian disobedience would not matter. We would have a free, one-way ticket to heaven regardless of how we lived. But Jesus' gospel is the Good News of the kingdom.[2] He taught that the messianic day had arrived. Therefore, in the power of the Holy Spirit, he said his disciples could now live the costly, life-giving standards of this dawning kingdom. That means living as he lived.

This urgent call to imitate Christ rather than the world runs throughout the New Testament. "Do not conform to the evil desires you had when you lived in ignorance," Peter pleads with his readers. "But just as he who called you is holy, so be holy in all you do; for it is written: 'Be holy, because I am holy'" (1 Peter 1:14–16).

Paul urged the Corinthian Christians to "follow my example, as I follow the example of Christ" (1 Cor. 11:1). A call to Christ-centered nonconformity begins the long ethical section of Paul's most theological letter, Romans, in which he begs the Roman Christians to turn from the world and surrender their total selves unconditionally to Christ: "Do not conform any longer to the pattern of this world" (Rom. 12:2).

The apostles urged the early Christians to imitate Jesus—and especially his sacrificial love on the cross—in the family, the church, and society. "Husbands, love your wives, just as Christ loved the church" (Eph. 5:25). Jesus' example is also the norm for the congregation. Paul pleaded with the Philippian Christians to be gentle, loving, humble, and compassionate: "Your attitude should be the same as that of Christ Jesus" (Phil. 2:5). Peter's instruction to slaves shows that even in the marketplace, Jesus' example is the standard: "If you suffer for doing good and you endure it, this is commendable before God. To this you were called, because Christ suffered for you, leaving you an example, that you should follow in his steps" (1 Peter 2:20–21). Persistently, consistently, the New Testament summons Christians to imitate Jesus.

Still, the modern church prefers to accept only half of Jesus. They willingly accept him either as model or as mediator—but not both. Some urge us to follow his example of love and social concern, but they forget about his cross. Others emphasize his death for our sins, but fail to imitate his actions. But Christianity is strong only when we embrace the whole Christ.

Following Christ is not some vague, abstract idea, some lofty philosophical concept. It means living like Jesus. If the New Testament is true, then Jesus longs for us to love our neighbors the way he did—daily, persistently, practically. Jesus modeled servanthood, self-sacrifice, and special concern for the poor and neglected. And he also cared for people's spiritual needs.

All that sounds foreign to modern ears because we are not accustomed to denying ourselves in order to serve others. But Jesus insisted that discipleship is impossible without self-denial. Instant gratification is at the core of modern life. Costly self-denial is at the center of Jesus' way. We must choose. "If any want to become my followers, let them deny themselves and take up their cross and follow me. For those who want to save their life will lose it, and those who lose their life for my sake, and for the sake of the gospel, will save it" (Mark 8:34–35 NRSV). That is why serious Christians today are gentle, but uncompromising, nonconformists.

The very thought of self-denial grates on modern hearts. They prefer the quick fix delusion of instant gratification. That attitude is behind our runaway divorce rates and abortion on demand—it is too tough and costly to learn mutual submission in marriage and care for inconvenient, unexpected babies. It is behind Wall Street scandals and environmental destruction—it takes too long to earn money honestly and wisely. It is behind government deficits billed to our grandchildren—we want everything now for ourselves even if we cannot pay for it.

Jesus has a better way, and it leads to far deeper joy and happiness than instant sex and wealth can ever bring. But there is no way around the cross.

Jesus also refused to follow the customs of his world in other ways. In fact, he was such an uncompromising nonconformist that the authorities angrily decided to destroy him (Luke 19:45–47). Notice the many ways Jesus was different.

- To violent revolutionaries who wanted to throw out the oppressive Roman conquerors with the sword, Jesus said, "Love your enemies" (Matt. 5:44)

- To powerful rulers who loved to dominate their sub-jects, Jesus called for servant leaders (Matt. 20:25–26)
- To wealthy people who neglected the poor, Jesus warned that failure to feed the hungry leads to eter-nal damnation (Matt. 25:41)
- To men happy with the easy divorce laws of the day (easy for men, that is), Jesus declared that the Cre-ator's will for marriage is a man and woman joyfully joined together in lifelong covenant

One striking mark of Jesus' radical difference was his spe-cial concern for the poor and marginalized. A central part of his mission on earth was "to preach good news to the poor ... proclaim freedom for the prisoners and recovery of sight for the blind, [and] to release the oppressed" (Luke 4:18). He praised Zaccheus for giving half of his wealth to the poor. He warned of the dangers of riches: "It is easier for a camel to go through the eye of a needle than for a rich man to enter the kingdom of God" (Luke 18:25). Of course, Jesus loved the rich just as much as the poor. He gladly invited everyone to repent and join his new community. But when the rich did join him, Jesus expected them to follow his and Zac-cheus' example of costly sharing with the needy.

Jesus had a special concern for lepers, prostitutes, and disabled people. While most of his contemporaries de-manded that lepers keep their distance, Jesus gently touched them and healed them. Some religious leaders explicitly excluded the disabled from the religious com-munity. Jesus taught that his kingdom was for "the poor, the crippled, the blind and the lame" (Luke 14:21).

He dramatically defied his culture's attitudes toward women. To Jesus' contemporaries it was a scandal for a man to appear with a woman in public. One rabbi taught that it was better to burn a copy of the Torah (the five books of Moses) than to allow a woman to touch it, and in a widely used prayer, Jewish men thanked God they were not Gentiles, slaves, or women!

Jesus and his new community rejected centuries of male prejudice and treated women as equals. He appeared with women in public (John 4:27), and taught them theology (Luke 10:38–42). He allowed a woman that everybody knew was a sinner to wash his feet with her tears, wipe them with her long hair, kiss and perfume them–and in public (Luke 7:36–50)! When Mary abandoned her traditional role of cooking food to listen to Jesus' theology lesson, Martha objected. But Jesus defended Mary (Luke 10:38–42). It was surely no accident that Jesus granted the first resurrection appearance to women!

In its attitude toward women, the early church continued to live Jesus' messianic challenge to the status quo. The prophets had promised that when the Messiah came, both daughters and sons, both women and men would prophesy (Joel 2:28). That happened in the early church. Women prophesied (Acts 21:9; 1 Cor. 11:5) and corrected the theology of men (Acts 18:24–26). Liberated from the restrictions of the synagogue, women participated enthusiastically in the early church's worship services. Paul even joyously boasted that in Christ, there is "neither Jew nor Greek, slave nor free, male nor female" (Gal. 3:28).

Even if you object to women as ordained church leaders, you cannot escape the radical message from Jesus that women should never be treated as second-class citizens. This is not secular feminism but biblical Christianity.

What an astonishing upsetting of the status quo! Jesus and his new community of women and men, rich and poor, were indeed a new kind of society that refused to conform to society's sin.

That is the concrete historical person in whose steps the New Testament calls Christians to follow. It is with reference to this specific man from Nazareth that Paul declares that we "are being transformed into his likeness with ever-increasing glory" (2 Cor. 3:18).

Why do serious Christians regularly look into the face of God and beg to become more like this first-century Galilean? Because we know him. Because we know who he really is and because we know him personally.

Christians know that the carpenter from Nazareth is also the second person of the Trinity, the only Son of God. The one who healed the sick and cared for the poor is the Eternal Word who from the beginning was with God and was God (John 1:1). The one who associated with lepers and prostitutes was the One who flung the stars into space. The one who treated women with such dignity and respect and insisted on fidelity in marriage was the Eternal Word become flesh.

The same apostles who summon us to pattern our lives after this Jesus fell on their faces to worship him. He is the One to whom every knee should bow and every tongue confess (Phil. 2:10–11). He is the One in whom "God was pleased to have all his fullness dwell" (Col. 1:19).

If the carpenter from Nazareth were only a wise teacher, then we could sort through his ethical advice, picking and choosing what feels good to us. But since we know that he is truly King of kings and Lord of lords, we can only fall on our knees in worship and pray for the power to live as he lived.

To be sure, if we only knew *about* him, if we only knew that the Eternal Word commands us to be holy as he is holy, then our knowledge would be a terrifying law. But we truly, personally, know him. We don't just know about him. By faith, we have a living, personal relationship with him. We know that this perfect model is all-sufficient Redeemer who forgives us when we falter. With Paul we declare that he now lives in our hearts and minds: "I no longer live, but Christ lives in me" (Gal. 2:20). We confess with glad astonishment that the same divine power that raised Jesus from the dead is now at work in each of our imperfect personalities reshaping us into the pattern of the man from Nazareth (Eph. 1:18–2:6). The one who offers the model also provides the strength.

Have you ever observed a little boy who looked up to a famous athlete? As he watches that superstar, he tries to walk like him, talk like him, even dress like him. In a way, that's how we should approach Jesus–only Jesus, through his Spirit, empowers us to live up to his example.

Think of what would happen if only a small fraction of today's Christians truly lived like this wondrous Lord. That first little band of 120 men and women did just that. In the power of the Spirit, they sought to live like Jesus rather than the society around them, and as astonished observers asked for explanations, they eagerly shared the gospel. And the world changed.

In spite of the sad conformity of so many Christians, a daring minority still seeks to embrace the full biblical Christ today. When they do, his resurrection power blazes forth, transforming persons, neighborhoods, and societies. Examples are everywhere:

- A wealthy Australian businessman lives among the poor and discovers how to make 75,000 small loans that have dramatically improved the lot of 375,000 people in just thirteen years.

- A Denver pastor urges a small middle-class congregation to unleash the laity and move beyond the walls of the church in evangelism and social concern and the congregation explodes from one hundred to one thousand in about ten years.

- A gifted Indian leader fresh from graduate study at Cambridge decides to live and work among the poor to share Jesus' whole gospel. The result is new Christians, new churches, and a ministry serving 50,000 people.[3] When people live and preach like Jesus, the world is transformed.

I'll never forget watching Mother Teresa address the National Prayer Breakfast in Washington in February 1994. She was a tiny, frail woman. Even with a special stand, her bobbing head was barely visible above the podium. But the President of the United States, leading members of Congress, prominent politicians from many countries, and thousands of leaders from across the globe listened silently in rapt attention as she talked about the poor and the sanctity of human life. She commanded no troops and displayed no oratorical brilliance. But her words had power because we all knew she lives like Jesus.

For many years I prayed regularly for the Spirit-filled gift of working biblically for justice and peace. Then a few years ago, I incorporated that request in a broader prayer. I began to ask God regularly for the Spirit-filled gift of combining evangelism and social transformation.

Today I just pray to become more like Jesus—and to learn how, in the power of the Spirit, to help the church become more like him. Frequently as I spend quiet time in the Lord's presence, my mind turns to 2 Corinthians 3:18. I feel overwhelmed with the fact that I can look deep into the face of the Lord of the universe. And I beg him, sometimes with tears, to transform me day by day, more and more into his very likeness. Again and again, too, I plead for the Spirit's wisdom and power to be an instrument to help the church become more like our Lord.

I have not arrived. I often fail. So I understand my sisters and brothers who also let him down. Together we rest in his mercy.

But my deepest longing is to be part of an ever growing circle of committed disciples who truly reflect his glory. I know what would happen. Revival would break out. Non-Christians would come to faith. Broken homes would discover new joy and wholeness. A new passion for justice and freedom, life and peace, would penetrate the tough corridors of economic and political power. The world would change. And millions of new people would discover the unspeakable joy of knowing that no matter what happens now, they will sing and dance forever in the presence of the risen Lord.

All we have to do is let Jesus become the central passion of our life. Above everything else, we must long to be more and more like him and less like the world.

3

RENEWING MARRIAGE AND FAMILY

Characteristic Three

Genuine Christians keep their marriage covenants and put children before career

I want to tell you about my Uncle Jesse and Aunt Lydia, the woman he loved.[1]

After five years of happy marriage, tragedy struck Lydia and Jesse's home. The day after the birth of their second daughter mental illness invaded their lives. Lydia became increasingly disoriented and unstable. Eventually she lost touch with reality almost completely. It became increasingly impossible for Jesse to care for her at home. Finally, after several years of pain and struggle, Jesse had to take Lydia to a psychiatric hospital in Hamilton, Ontario. At first, he checked with the doctors each week when he visited, believing his wife would soon be better.

"Your wife is not going to get any better," the doctor announced one day. "I think you should go home and start over. Take care of your girls, and forget about this woman."

"Well, Doc," Jesse said, "I can go home and take care of the girls, but I can't forget Lydia. She's part of me."

For almost thirty years, Jesse drove two hours to Hamilton every two or three weeks to visit the woman he had promised to love for better or worse till death parted them.

"Usually she was glad to see me," Jesse says. "Sometimes, though, she would say she hoped I broke my neck on the way home. When that happened I'd go home and think, 'Well, what am I going to do? No use me going up there anymore.'"

"And then I couldn't help but think about her. And in a week or two I'd be back up again, and I could get an entirely different response."

For many years, Jesse hoped and prayed that God would heal his wife. "Why she couldn't get healed, I don't know. That's one of the mysteries of this life."

In 1953, the doctors suggested a lobotomy (an operation in which a lobe of the brain is cut).

When Uncle Jesse saw her the next day, he marveled at the change in her. She asked questions about home and other things she hadn't talked about in years.

Jesse tried bringing Lydia home for a week or two, but it didn't work well. Once she wandered away and walked to my parents' farm about four miles away.

"Some people were scared of her. It was a long pull there," Jesse told me.

My dad went along when Jesse sadly returned her to the hospital.

Months later, he brought her home again. This time, things went much better. The doctors had been testing various kinds of medication for Lydia and had finally found the right combination. After twenty-nine years, she was home again.

Her sloppy appearance and religious indifference were painful reminders that Lydia was not the woman Jesse once knew, but she was reasonable and cooperative.

For three years Jesse gently cared for the woman he still thought of as his youthful sweetheart and bride.

Then one Thursday, Lydia got sick to her stomach. A few days later, her appendix ruptured. Because of the lobotomy, she never felt the pain that would have warned her that something was wrong.

"Would you pray for me?" Lydia asked.

"I'm sure she was a Christian before her mind got warped," Jesse said, "but afterward she could think most anything. While she was home those last years, she never showed any spiritual emotion, that I could see. And now she said, 'Would you pray for me?'

"I said, 'Sure, I'll pray for you.' The next day she died. I felt this was the Lord's time to take her home. It all went so peacefully."

I cried as I listened to Uncle Jesse tell the story of his marriage. "Did you ever feel angry at the Lord?" I asked.

"I did right at first," he replied. "I thought, This isn't fair—she was twenty-nine years old when this happened. But that doesn't get you anyplace.

"All those years, never once did I feel that she was a burden. Oh, she was a burden, but I never felt it was anything I should be relieved of. I loved her, and I did all I could."

"Do you think it would be harder today to do what you did?" I asked. "Thirty years back, divorce was seldom heard of, but today men abandon wives for far less reason."

"I can't understand the modern attitude," Uncle Jesse said quietly. "I chose a wife who I thought was it. Now why, after ten years, would I want to get rid of her for somebody else?"

"It looks like you've been asked to walk a difficult road," I suggested softly.

"Yes, especially if I had seen those thirty years ahead," he replied. "I took her to the hospital with the feeling that she would be returning in three months or so. It just didn't work that way. We walk with the Lord one day at a time."

Uncle Jesse made a vow before God with the woman he loved to live in lifelong covenant for better or for worse. It got worse. But he kept that covenant, by God's grace, one day at a time.

Today's world feels like another planet. Adultery drives a sword through many marriages. In the United States, half of all recent marriages will dissolve in divorce.[2] Increasing numbers of couples don't even bother to get married. Almost one-third of all children in the United States today are born to single parents. Less than 50 percent of the children in the United States will spend their full childhood living with both their mother and father. Anguish and tragedy stalk our homes in the form of abuse. We are doing to our children what no civilization in human history has ever done.

Careful scientific studies now prove what the Creator always knew. Children need their parents—both of them. Children of divorced or unmarried parents suffer. In a trend-setting essay entitled "Dan Quayle Was Right," published in the *Atlantic Monthly,* Barbara Dafoe Whitehead recently summarized the shocking statistics:

Children in single-parent families are six times as likely to be poor. They are also likely to stay poor longer. Twenty-two percent of children in one-parent families will experience poverty during childhood for seven years or more, as compared with only 2 percent of children in two-parent families. . . . Children in single-parent families are two to three times as likely as children in two-parent families to have emotional and behavioral problems. They are also more likely to drop out of high school, to get pregnant as teenagers, to abuse drugs, and to be in trouble with the law. . . . Many children from disrupted families have a harder time achieving intimacy in relationships, forming a stable marriage, or even holding a steady job.[3]

Our society cannot survive for long with such pain and brokenness at the center of family life.

I remember a beautiful song composed by Clyde Hollinger called "You Don't Have to Fear the Storm." He wrote it for his little son who was terrified one stormy evening by the crack and roar of thunder. In the song, Clyde tells how he took his little boy in his arms, held him tightly, and softly promised: "Son, you don't have to fear the storm, I will be with you all the time, you can trust my word."[4] Half the fathers and mothers today cannot honestly sing that song. You cannot promise always to be there if you leave open the option of walking away from marriage when things get tough.

If Christians today followed Jesus rather than the world in our marriages and sexual practices, the Christian family would stand out in stunning starkness and appealing beauty. It would be like a cozy inviting living room warmed by a crackling fireplace in a frigid city paralyzed by a raging blizzard. Sadly, disobediently, Christians break their marriage vows almost as often as their non-Christian neighbors.[5]

God forbid that my words cause anyone more pain. I weep over the anguish and torment of those who have been divorced. I know temptation and hardship bombard every marriage. I know many people face enormous hurt and horrendously difficult spouses in ways that I can hardly even imagine. I certainly believe that the Christian community should support those who rightly separate for an appropriate time from an abusive spouse. And no matter what our sin, God stands eager to forgive all who repent.

But so many married couples give up too easily. Cheap divorce is widespread. In a recent movie, a father tried to help his little son understand why mom and dad were getting divorced. "Mothers and fathers just walk through the same doors at different times," the departing father explained. His little son's response speaks for millions of lonely, hurting kids: "Then why don't they wait for each other?"[6]

How have we gotten into such a tragedy? What has produced the highest divorce rate in human history? There are lots of reasons. Many things have conspired together to make lifelong marriage harder now than it was for our grandparents.

New ideas broadcast everywhere with the persuasive power of modern media have undermined sexual integrity and marriage covenant. Modern intellectuals endorsed relativism, claiming that one ethical idea is as good as another. Then the sexual revolution of the sixties spread the poison everywhere. Abstinence before marriage was mocked as puritan prudery. Open marriage and "loving" adultery are just two of many lifestyle choices served up by the modern ethical supermarket and made "safe" by contraceptive technology. Every individual should seek their own self-fulfillment. If a spouse no longer meets your needs, some people think, you owe it to yourself to find someone who does. Personal self-realization overrides marriage covenant and parental responsibility.

Other changes have also been at work. Beneath the revolution in values lie powerful changes in the economy. I grew up on a farm where my mom and dad worked together and parented together seven days a week. That was the normal pattern through much of human history until the industrial revolution in the early nineteenth century. Then work and family separated. Men left home to work in factories and offices miles from home where mother was left alone to care for the children. The model of a breadwinning father working outside the home while a nurturing mother does almost all the parenting by herself is a modern development produced by the industrial revolution. One tragic result was that fathers lost many of their parenting opportunities and children lost close emotional ties with their fathers.

Modern science and technology also undermined the family in other ways. Previously, people usually lived in one community all their life, surrounded by relatives and friends who supported their marriage. With modern education, scientific specialization, and easy transportation, people began to move all around the country and even the world to find a job that fit their specialized skills. In the new location, the isolated nuclear family had far less community support for keeping marriage vows or sacrificing for children. At the same time fast food restaurants, microwave meals, and television destroyed regular family dinners—even for the nuclear family.

The material abundance produced by the industrial revolution seduced us still further. People became so preoccupied with more and more gadgets, products, and luxuries that they neglected personal relationships. Making money became more important than spending time with spouse and children.

Faithful marriage and wholesome family life are much harder today than they were for our grandparents. That does not mean they are impossible. In fact, if our society is to survive, we must do whatever it takes to restore marriage and family. But to do that, we will have to challenge not only our culture's ethical relativism, sexual promiscuity, and easy divorce—we will also have to reject materialism and demand that our economic institutions serve the family rather than undermine it.

Knowing all the powerful weapons Satan uses to attack marriage should give us tender hearts for broken people. We need to stand and weep with those who have failed, serving as the gentle messengers of God's overflowing forgiveness. God have mercy if those of us who have not experienced divorce give in to the temptation to be proud, self-righteous, and judgmental. If we are honest we know very well that we all face the same temptations. We all have walked close to the precipice. But we need not despair. Christian faith has the resources to restore the family and the joy of lifelong marriage covenant—if we are willing to surrender unconditionally to God's way.

Three biblical truths are essential: Covenant must replace contract; the cross of self-sacrifice must replace personal self-realization; and individualism must give way to community so that the church can offer powerful communal support to marriage and families. These three—covenant, cross, and church community—are the essential Cs for Christian marriage.

First of all, *covenant*. What is the biblical understanding of the marriage covenant? Genesis 2 and Matthew 19 help us understand. Genesis 2 is a fantastic story. Adam was not satisfied with the plants and animals and the things he could make. So God brings him Eve, bone of his bone, flesh of his flesh. Adam says, "Wow! That's what I've been looking for!" And their delight in each other was very good. The Bible says that the man and the woman became one flesh. They became one, permanently.

Matthew 19 helps us see more clearly what God was telling us in Genesis: Marriage is for life. It is a lifelong commitment. In Matthew 19, Jesus responds to a question about divorce. Quoting Genesis 2:24, Jesus says they become "one." The Greek text actually says "one flesh." And then in verse 6 Jesus insists: "What God has joined together, let no one separate" (NRSV). Let no person tear apart this divinely established covenant of lifelong unity. Marriage is not just for good times; it is for bad times too. It is "for better, for worse, for richer, for poorer, for sickness and health, till death do us part."

Only when we understand the setting in Jesus' day do we grasp the full force of Jesus' teaching. In first-century Palestine, divorce was easy—at least for a man. A clear law of Moses (Deut. 24:1) gave the husband a great deal of freedom to dismiss his wife. Jesus explicitly sets aside the Mosaic law and returns to the Creator's original plan. "It was because you were so hard-hearted that Moses allowed you to divorce your wives, but from the beginning it was not so" (Matt. 19:8 NRSV). In Jesus' dawning kingdom, the disciples of Jesus should and can keep marriage vows the way the Creator originally intended.

Frequently, Jesus relaxed rigid ethical rules of his time. But here in the case of divorce he did just the opposite. To be sure, he permitted divorce in the one case of marital unfaithfulness (Matt. 19:9). But his teaching clearly, pointedly excludes divorce for the vast majority of reasons people today abandon their spouses.

Jesus' standard is high. Large parts of the modern church flatly defy Jesus' teaching. Christians cannot hope to restore the family unless we are ready to return to the Creator's design. Are Christian couples today ready to follow Jesus rather than conform to the world? It will not be easy, but it is the only way to restore the family and recover the deepest joy in marriage.

At some point, the storms of life will roar through every marriage like a raging tornado. The best protection against giving up at that point is to be committed without reservation for the rest of one's life—"till death do us part." If that is clear then we will struggle, we will cry, we will pray and trust God to bring us through.

The world has a cheap substitute for Christian marriage covenant. It is called contract. Sometimes the contract is explicit. Some couples approaching marriage actually work out a written contract. They agree on what each party will do. If the one party breaks the agreement and fails to keep their promises then it is okay to dissolve the marriage because it is just a contract. More often the contract is implicit. We do not say explicitly that it is just a contract but it is. We say, "Let's try it. Let's see if it works. Let's see if it feels good. Let's see if it meets my needs." Behind those words, of course, is the hidden assumption of contract and the lie that self-realization should be our highest priority. If the other party does not meet my needs then the contract is broken. If I do not enjoy self-fulfillment, then the contract is off.

Society's limited marriage contract is not Christian covenant. It is the devil's cheap substitute. It is a fraud, a trick. Satan, of course, sells it to us with slick language and big promises. He says it brings freedom. He argues: "Society changes; you change; how on earth can you make a life-long covenant?" I want to shout to my children, to all of our children, to all of us: "Let us not be deceived by Satan's lousy substitute." Let us choose unconditional, solemn covenant made in the presence of the living God rather than a limited liability contract. In God's name, let us choose Christian partners who share that biblical understanding. And then, like Uncle Jesse, let's keep our vows, no matter what the world says and does. That is the only foundation strong enough to bring us the deep joy of continuing growth and lasting love over a lifetime of mutual submission and sacrifice. Covenant, biblical covenant before God, is the foundation of Christian marriage.

The second C is the *cross*. Anybody that has been married a few months knows there is pain as well as joy in marriage. We are all proud, petty, selfish sinners. We hurt each other, and then silly and stupid as we are, we try to cover it up or blame our spouse. We refuse to say we are sorry. Even in the best of marriages, we hurt each other deeply. Finally, there is only one solution for that. It is a costly solution. It is the mystery at the heart of the gospel. It is the cross. It is costly forgiveness.

Ephesians 5 says that husbands should love their wives the way Christ loved the church. (I'm sure Christ wants wives to do the same for their husbands.) How does Christ love the church? He died for us. He put aside short-term self-fulfillment and embraced the agony of Roman crucifixion. Why? Not because we were so good. He did it because he loved us so much that he gladly sacrificed himself to bring us unconditional forgiveness.

That kind of costly love is absolutely essential for lifelong, joyful marriage. Betrayal, sin, and anguish will invade every marriage. At that point, as we saw in chapter 1, there is one good option and two bad ones.

One misguided choice is to let resentment and anger take control. Eventually that will destroy the relationship.

Another wrong choice is to pretend it really does not matter much. "Aw, shucks. It was nothing. In fact, I have already forgotten it." That of course, is a lie. Pretense and cheap grace simply cannot restore reconciliation and intimacy.

Costly forgiveness is the only choice that really works. That is the way of the cross. Pain, betrayal, selfishness, and sin in marriage do matter. They hurt like crazy. They tear us apart. Costly forgiveness responds to the hurt in marriage the same way that God responds to sin. Sin is damnably serious. But at the cross, God embraces the punishment we deserve because God loves us in spite of our sinful failures.

That kind of costly forgiveness is the only way to stay happily married for a lifetime. When betrayal comes, we need to deal with it. We need to face clearly the full agony of this vicious javelin thrust to our heart. Sin needs to be confessed. Genuine repentance is essential. Then in time, by God's grace, we can also add: "Because I love you, I accept the pain of your betrayal and I forgive you." That is the only way for husbands and wives to rediscover reconciliation and joy after betrayal. You cannot pretend that you have not been hurt. You cannot wish it away. You can only embrace the pain and forgive. As repentance and forgiveness strengthen and reinforce each other, healing and reconciliation slowly grow.

How often do we need to embrace the cross in our marriages? Husbands are to love their wives and wives are to love their husbands as Christ loves the church. How often does Christ forgive you? Seventy times seven and seventy times seven. How many times has Christ forgiven you in the past year? In the last ten years? In the last fifty years? That is the way that we need to go on forgiving our husbands and our wives.

That does not mean spouses should overlook persistent patterns of abuse and other sinful behavior. Rather than becoming co-dependent enablers, we must confront wrong. When separation becomes necessary, the Christian family should walk with both parties nurturing repentance, healing, and eventually reconciliation.

Costly forgiveness is closely related to covenant. The cross means never giving up. As long as we live, Christ stands before us offering forgiveness. God does not say, "I have had enough of you. I have had enough of your failures, stupidity, unfaithfulness, and sin." As long as we live God stands there pleading: "I want to give you another chance." Taking the way of the cross in our marriages, loving our spouses as Christ loved the church, means not giving up, even in the difficult, painful times.

This is not, I hasten to add, a recipe for agony and masochism. It is the only way to healing and joy. It is the only way to lasting happiness in marriage. Since pain and failure will always come, even in the best of marriages, the only way to restoration and wholeness is costly forgiveness. The cross is central to Christian marriage.

A third crucial element *Christian* marriages need is genuine *community* in the church. Young people may think: "All this sounds scary. The demands seem very high." That is true. It is also true that the rewards are even greater. But when a lifelong commitment seems hard, Christians remember that we are not alone. In addition to the daily presence of the Spirit, Christians enjoy the love and support of the church. All of the other brothers and sisters in the body of Christ promise to help us. That is why we have church weddings rather than just going off by ourselves to elope. The wedding covenant is not merely a solemn pledge between God and two persons. It is also a communal vow witnessed by our brothers and sisters in Christ. By attending the wedding, they all pledge to help us in our marriage covenant.

In Christ's body, if one suffers, all suffer. If one rejoices, all rejoice (1 Cor. 12:26). That means celebrating weddings and fiftieth anniversaries together in the body of Christ. It also means standing together in the tough times. That is what we promise every young couple we watch walk down the aisle to be married in the church. We are responsible for each other's marriages. Everybody in a congregation is responsible if somebody's marriage fails. Did we pray or gossip? Did we cry or silently sneer? Did we gently counsel holding on or did we stay coldly silent? Did we offer costly help or let them struggle alone?

There are numerous ways that the Christian community could strengthen marriage and family. We need much more teaching for our children and youth about the beauty and joy of lifelong commitment in marriage. We need more premarital counseling. I wish that every church would announce that it will not marry anyone unless they have gone through several months of Christian marriage counseling. We also need better post-marital counseling. We need to share our marriage struggles in small fellowship groups and encourage each other to get counseling when necessary.

It is very easy to be too proud to do that. God has blessed Arbutus and me with a long, joyous marriage. As I related in chapter 1, there came a time when we very badly needed expert help. I must confess that I was too proud to do that for quite a while. I knew that many marriages around us were in trouble and needed help. In fact, I was encouraging some of them to go for counseling! But me? Finally, when I hurt enough, I agreed. Thank God for those six months of marriage counseling with a gifted Christian therapist.

Satan is a clever liar. He says marriages used to last because people had no other option. They hated each other, lived parallel lives, and only stayed together because of custom. Now that is partly true and partly false. But Christian community provides a solution to the truth in this charge. I do not believe God wants us to endure continuing agony in our marriages. A church that genuinely understands what it means to be the body of Christ will find ways to help each other work at the pain, the failures, the hurts in each of our marriages. Unless the church is ready to invest large amounts of money and time in helping its members discover new joy and wholeness in their marriages, it should not criticize the world or pretend that it has an alternative to the sexual and marital tragedy all around us. But the church today does know a better way. We know that lasting, fulfilling marriage starts with biblical covenant, is renewed by costly forgiveness, and is strengthened by the warm embrace of loving sisters and brothers in Christ.

Thus far, I have talked mostly about what Christians can do within the community of believers. But the larger culture could also significantly strengthen marriage and the family. Think of how different it would be if the influential people in art, education, and the media supported rather than mocked sexual integrity and marital fidelity. Imagine a situation where most people spoke and lived the truth that parents ought to be more concerned with parenting than career or wealth. Consider how much easier it would be if employers supported parental leave for new mothers and fathers and offered flex-time to encourage parenting and caring for the elderly. Even the right government programs (such as tax laws that favor marriage over cohabitation) could play a modest but significant role in strengthening marriage.

Fortunately, there are new signs of hope today in both church and society. For the first time in decades influential secular authorities are talking openly about the fact that children need both parents. More and more people are endorsing sexual abstinence until marriage. Broad coalitions like the National Fatherhood Initiative are summoning fathers to renewed responsibility. And one of the main themes in the Million Man March was for men to go back to their wives and children as committed husbands and fathers.

Within the Christian community, the pro-family movement has grown strong. New organizations like Promise Keepers are calling Christian men to be faithful husbands and available, caring fathers. Campaigns like True Love Waits are inspiring hundreds of thousands of Christian youth to sign pledges of virginity until marriage.

All that is promising. But it is only a beginning. Just imagine the impact if even a quarter of today's Christians modeled joyful Christian marriages and families for the next two decades. There are few things that would have more evangelistic impact upon our world so full of broken homes.

I pray for tens of millions of Christian families whose joy and wholeness stand out in stark contrast to the surrounding darkness. In those homes husbands and wives know that the best thing they can do for their children is to love and care for each other. They take the time and invest the energy to communicate honestly, repent when they fail, forgive each other, grow together, find delight in each other, and submit to each other. They treasure family time more than promotions. They keep their vows even in the tough times. Their joyful, wholesome families demonstrate powerfully that the Creator's design for sex and marriage is finally the only way to enduring happiness, peace, and yes, self-fulfillment.

Living models of that kind of joy and integrity would be a powerful witness in the midst of the pain in families today. Neighbors would watch carefully. Slowly, after making sure the joy is genuine, they would often seek the same wholeness and gladly embrace the same Lord.

In the next two decades, Christian marriage could become one of our most powerful means of evangelism. Today's hurting, broken families long for something better. We can offer them what they seek. But only if we first live it. Will enough Christians today follow Jesus rather than the world? Will enough Christians model such fidelity, joy, and wholeness in our marriages and families that the world will see and believe?

That can only happen family by family, person by person. God helping me, I pledge to treasure my wife and my children above work, money, and fame. They have been God's best gift to me after his Son.

4

IMMERSED IN PRAYER, FILLED WITH THE SPIRIT

Characteristic Four

Genuine Christians nurture daily spiritual renewal and live in the power of the Spirit

Almost everybody I know feels guilty about how little time they spend in daily devotions. Somehow finding time for regular prayer and devotional reading seems especially hard today. Partly it is the frantic pace of modern life. Partly it is the prevailing secularism that sneaks subtly into our hearts.

At one level, neglecting prayer should be absurdly wrongheaded. The greatest Christians of the ages all tell us how important it was to them. Our Lord and Savior makes utterly astounding promises to those who pray. Still we struggle to squeeze out a few minutes for prayer.

I am no exception. For years I felt guilty about how little time I set aside for prayer. Theoretically, theologically, I knew it was important. I even wrote about it! At the beginning of Evangelicals for Social Action I wrote that nothing would be more important for the recovery of biblical social concern than prayer. Even then, I still did not find the time. Each morning the pile of "important, urgent" things was so great that I could hardly force myself to spare ten minutes. Even when I did, my mind was often preoccupied with waiting responsibilities.

Like everybody else, I suppose, I comforted myself with the reminder to avoid legalism. It is not a sin to miss a day here and there. Then it dawned on me that when you are missing six mornings out of seven, legalism is no longer your problem.

Finally God used tough love to get my attention. Earlier, I talked about a hard time in my marriage. The only way I survived was by pleading each morning with the Lord to give me the strength to get through the day. Those times of talking to God about my pain, begging for forgiveness, and asking for strength became times of deep comfort. I began to enjoy my daily conversations with my Lord in a way I never had before. During that time and since, it has been much easier to set time aside at the beginning of the day for personal devotions.

Of course, our whole day of activity should be a life of prayer in which we pray without ceasing. It is wonderful to learn how to live at two levels. At one level we can be driving the car or talking on the phone. At another level we can be breathing short prayers to God for ourselves and others. But it is also true that nothing takes the place of regular times set aside exclusively for conversation with our Divine Lover.

A friend of mine, Peter Schreck, underscores this point with a personal story. One day Peter listened with growing dismay to a group of Christian faculty debating learnedly about prayer. One professor argued that there was no need to set aside a special time just for prayer since all of life can be a prayer. In response, Peter reflected on his relationship with his wife, Carol, during the preceding month. They had been frantically busy moving all their belongings across the continent. "I was married to Carol during the whole month of August," Peter said. "But it was very important for us to stop our harried labor once in a while and go for a walk together in the moonlight." Regular time alone with God is essential.

Tough times can teach us the importance of prayer. So should the example of great Christians and the promises of Jesus.

William Wilberforce was the leader in the great British crusade to abolish the slave trade and slavery. Historians tell us that he and his colleagues, in a little circle called the Clapham Sect, immersed their political strategizing and lobbying in daily three-hour sessions of intercessory prayer. Later in the nineteenth century, Lord Shaftesbury spearheaded numerous social reforms, ending child labor and reforming the factories. When his son asked how he could do so many things at once, he replied: "By hearty prayer to Almighty God before I begin, by entering into it with faith and zeal, and by making my end to be His glory and the good of mankind."[1]

Evangelist Charles Finney—the "Billy Graham of the nineteenth century" and also a leading crusader against slavery—insisted that long hours of intercessory prayer were central to his work. Finney would have appreciated what Thielicke has said of Martin Luther. He prayed four hours each day, "not despite his busy life, but because only so could he accomplish his gigantic labors."[2] If some of the greatest Christians of the ages consider extensive prayer absolutely essential, are we not incredibly foolish to neglect it?

Believing Jesus knew what he was talking about will also strengthen our desire to pray more. In Mark 11:23–24, we have these incredible words: "I tell you the truth, if anyone says to this mountain, 'Go, throw yourself into the sea,' and does not doubt in his heart but believes that what he says will happen, it will be done for him. Therefore I tell you, whatever you ask for in prayer, believe that you have received it, and it will be yours."

The Gospel of John contains these breathtaking promises: "I tell you the truth, anyone who has faith in me will do what I have been doing. He will do even greater things than these, because I am going to the Father. And I will do whatever you ask in my name, so that the Son may bring glory to the Father. You may ask me for anything in my name, and I will do it" (14:12–14). "If you remain in me and my words remain in you, ask whatever you wish, and it will be given you" (15:7).

What more incentive do we need to pray regularly? Jesus himself took time away from his urgent ministry to talk alone with his heavenly Father. Then he made astounding promises to answer our prayers. If we know who Jesus is, how can we not make personal prayer a high priority?

Prayer is important because we are engaged in a life-and-death battle with Satan. Paul urges the Ephesians to "pray in the Spirit on all occasions with all kinds of prayers" (6:18). Why? Because he knows we are in a spiritual battle. "For our struggle is not against flesh and blood, but against the rulers, against the authorities, against the powers of this dark world and against the spiritual forces of evil in the heavenly realms" (v. 12). Who are the rulers and authorities? When Paul uses these words, he is talking about two closely related things. He is referring to evil social systems and distorted cultural values that twist and corrupt people. But Paul also means that behind these distorted human institutions lie demonic spiritual powers that fight against the Creator and seek to destroy the good creation God made. Therefore, Paul knows that in every encounter with twisted cultural values and social systems, we are also doing battle with the hosts of Satan. And Satan can only be defeated through prayer.

Spiritual warfare is important today. That does not mean we should spend time trying to draw detailed maps of the Satanic world or identify the name of every fallen angel. We do not have to engage in extrabiblical speculation about their names in order to bind them in the name of Jesus. Nor does it mean that we merely rebuke the demons of hunger, racism, and war and do nothing to change unjust social systems that foster poverty, apartheid, and violence. Biblical balance is what we need. That means both praying vigorously to bind the demonic powers and also working hard to reduce sex and violence in the media and reform unfair economic patterns.

Richard Lovelace has said that "most of those who are praying are not praying about social issues and most of those who are active in social issues are not praying very much."[3] If that is true, it is abominably wrongheaded and must change. Wilberforce prayed for the abolition of slavery, but at the same time he lobbied the Prime Minister to help make it happen. If we understand Paul's teaching on spiritual warfare, we will do the same.

We change history, both by our prayers and by our actions. In the old classic *With Christ in the School of Prayer*, Andrew Murray says that in prayer we are allowed to hold the hand that holds the destiny of the universe. Christians by their prayers "determine the history of this earth."[4] God wants to save the family. God wants everyone to hear the gospel. God wants more justice in society. And God wants to accomplish those things through our prayers.

How incredible! Prayer is not incidental to evangelism or peacemaking. Prayer is not peripheral to empowering the poor, protecting the unborn, and restoring the environment. Prayer is a central part of how we do those things. Andrew Murray puts it well: "As long as we look on prayer chiefly as the means of maintaining our own Christian life, we shall not know fully what it is meant to be. But when we learn to regard it as the highest part of the work entrusted to us, the root and strength of all other work, we shall see that there is nothing that we so need to study and practice as the art of praying aright."[5]

If prayer is that important, how can we make it more central in each of our lives? We can start where we are and develop a concrete, realistic plan. Don't try to go from ten minutes once a week to daily three-hour prayers! Open your heart to God and ask God to help you decide upon some modest increase–say ten or fifteen minutes at least five times a week if you have been skipping most days. Share your plan with a couple friends and ask them to check in a week to see how you are doing. After a few months, you can consider doing more.

I find it helpful to take a fairly lengthy quiet time several days a week. Then even on the busiest days, I try to begin with a much shorter time of quiet and prayer.

One of the greatest reasons for hope today is the powerful movements of prayer that are sweeping through the worldwide church.[6] If large numbers of Christians rediscover the power of prayer and open themselves fully to the blessed Holy Spirit, God will make the next century a time of evangelistic explosion and social transformation.

But it must start person by person–with you and me. I urge you to pray one minute each day for a week. Ask God what specific next step you should take in your prayer life. Perhaps just another five or ten minutes several times a week, or a thirty-minute time of prayer once a week with a few friends at work.

I dream of a new movement of Christians who immerse all their activity–not just their worship and evangelism but also their political analysis and cultural engagement—in all-night prayer meetings. I dream of a movement that thinks as it prays; that plans careful strategies as it surrenders to the Spirit; that prays for both miraculous signs and wonders and also effective social reform; that knows in its heart that nothing important will happen unless the Spirit blows through its plans; and also that God has no backup plan to use angels if we humans fail to do our part. A biblical combination of prayer and action will change the world.

Praying and depending on the Spirit are inseparable. It is because we are weak and needy that we plead with God to send the Holy Spirit sweeping through our hearts and minds. "In our day," Richard Foster says, "heaven and earth are on tiptoe waiting for the emergence of a Spirit-led, Spirit-intoxicated, Spirit-empowered people."[7] Why? Because without the Spirit, Christians fail. With the Spirit astonishing things happen.

That has certainly been true in the life of Dr. Kriengsak Chareonwongsak.[8] I first met him at Oxford at an international conference on Christian faith and economics. Dr. Kriengsak has been a professor of economics. He is also the leader of the fastest growing church in Thailand.

This unusual man grew up in a well-to-do Buddhist Thai family. Deeply moved by the plight of the poor, he was drawn to Marxism as he planned a political career. God had other plans. While studying in Australia, he was dramatically converted through the ministry of InterVarsity. A short time later, God overwhelmed him in the middle of the night with a powerful experience of the Spirit and the gift of tongues. A vision to plant a church in every one of the 685 districts of Thailand settled firmly in his heart. He completed his Ph.D. in economics, married a Thai student equally dedicated to evangelism, and returned to Bangkok in 1981.

Four months later, they started their first church, Hope of Bangkok. That Sunday and every Sunday since, someone has come to Christ in their worship service. Their growth has been breathtaking. Foreign missionaries had worked in Thailand for 170 years, but there were only about 70,000 Christians at the end of that time. In the last fifteen years, Dr. Kriengsak's Bangkok church has grown to over 13,000 members. They have also planted sister congregations in 285 districts. Forty thousand Thai Christians now worship in this expanding network of Hope of God churches.

What is their secret? Unusual leadership, excellent administration, and a good small group program all contribute. But Kriengsak attributes their success primarily to their special emphasis on both biblical authority and the presence and power of the Holy Spirit. Prayer, fasting, and miraculous signs and wonders have been a central feature of their evangelism and church life. Dr. Kriengsak is chairman of the Charismatic Fellowship of Asia. Dr. Kriengsak and the churches God has raised up through his ministry are certainly examples of what Richard Foster means by "Spirit-led, Spirit-intoxicated, Spirit-empowered people."

My friend Dr. Kriengsak is just one small part of the explosive story of the Pentecostal and charismatic renewal in the twentieth century.

Whatever else one may add, the most striking thing about this movement is its desire to be fully, unconditionally open to the Holy Spirit. To praise God for that is not to ignore weaknesses and excesses, nor is it to suggest that only Pentecostals and charismatics enjoy the fullness of the Spirit. The Holy Spirit dwells in all Christians. Through the centuries, some Christians from all traditions have surrendered themselves in unusual ways to the presence and power of the Spirit.

Something very unusual, however, started at the Azusa Street revival in Los Angeles in 1906. A black preacher named William J. Seymour led an interracial congregation that experienced the work of the Holy Spirit in dramatic, unexpected ways. The growing movement witnessed the kinds of miraculous signs and wonders described in the book of Acts. Evangelistic zeal and explosive growth followed. By 1970, there were seventy-two million. A mere twenty-two years later, they had grown by more than 500 percent to 410 million! Church statistician David Barrett estimates that by the year 2000, there will be 560 million Pentecostal and charismatic Christians.[9] Keep in mind that it took nineteen hundred years for the total number of Christians in the world to reach 558 million. So, in less than a hundred years, Pentecostal and charismatic Christians will have more than doubled that number! Surely the story of this Christian family demonstrates that God works wonders when his people open themselves to the Holy Spirit without reservation.

At this point, however, I should explain something: I have never spoken in tongues, nor have I personally witnessed a clear case of divine healing today. But since many of my friends enjoy those gifts, I am completely open, eager, and ready to receive any gifts the Holy Spirit chooses to send my way. At the same time, I feel no need to seek for the particular gifts of tongues or divine healing. What I desire with all my heart is the fullness and presence of the Holy Spirit every moment of my life. I long to be so unconditionally surrendered to God that absolutely nothing in me grieves or hinders the Spirit.

I wonder what would happen if the modern church took the Holy Spirit as seriously as Jesus and the apostles did. Jesus himself needed the Spirit to accomplish his mission (Matt. 12:28; Luke 4:1–18). As he prepared to leave his disciples, Jesus promised to send the Holy Spirit (John 14:15–18). Carefully, he instructed his little band to wait for the baptism of the Holy Spirit before they started on their incredible task to take Jesus' gospel to the ends of the earth (Acts 1:4–8). The Spirit, Jesus promised, would bring both power and guidance.

All through his letters, Paul makes it clear that it is simply impossible for us to live the way God desires apart from the power of the Spirit. In the flesh, using our own strength, we fail miserably. But when we walk by the Spirit, we make great progress in fulfilling "the righteous requirements of the law" (Rom. 8:1–4). "Live by the Spirit," Paul tells the Galatians, "and you will not gratify the desires of the sinful nature" (5:16). It is the Spirit who transforms us day by day into the very image of Christ (2 Cor. 3:18).

The fruit and gifts of the Holy Spirit are essential for the church. Paul expects those who belong to Christ to exhibit the fruit of the Spirit: "Love, joy, peace, patience, kindness, goodness, faithfulness, gentleness and self-control" (Gal. 5:22–23). I do not have to read very far down the list before I realize I cannot live that way by myself!

Several times, Paul listed the gifts of the Spirit that enable the body of Christ to carry on its ministry. "Now to each one the manifestation of the Spirit is given for the common good" (1 Cor. 12:7). Wisdom, knowledge, faith, gifts of healing, miraculous power, prophesy, distinguishing between good and evil spirits, speaking in tongues—"all these are the work of one and the same Spirit" (v. 11). The church needs all the Spirit's gifts to do God's work in the world.

Clearly, God wants Christians to be strong in the Spirit. But the proper understanding of this strength is crucial. Sometimes Christians want to possess and control this awesome divine power. Sometimes we even blasphemously try to use it for our own selfish purposes. Christian leaders are especially vulnerable to this temptation. I have discovered that precisely when the Spirit moves most powerfully through me when I preach, Satan sneaks in to whisper some nonsense in my ear: "That was really brilliant, Ron." Unless I quickly rebuke the old liar, I can easily fall into his trap and take credit for the Spirit's powerful presence. Few things are more dangerous for Christian leaders.

Ephesians 6:19 helps at just this point. Paul, the most famous Christian preacher of the centuries, asks people to pray so that he will find words when he tries to preach. "Pray also for me, that whenever I open my mouth, words may be given me so that I will fearlessly make known the mystery of the gospel." Now this would not be strange if the request came from some young seminary student frightened by his first sermon. But Paul? He had given thousands of sermons. He was good at that! But even this brilliant preacher knew that the power to speak faithfully for God was not something he controlled. Rather it was a divine gift that the Spirit bestowed moment by moment.

That is how we should pray to be strong in the Lord. That is the way we should understand the gifts that the Spirit bestows. They are not ours to possess and manipulate. Moment by moment as the Spirit grants us the power to live the Christian life and minister in Christ's body, we need to stand in awe of God's power. We must constantly remind ourselves and others that the glory belongs to God, not us. We must regularly recall that we remain strong only as long as we continue in faith, obedience, and humility. If Christians today will seek in that way for the power of the Spirit in all their work, the results will astound us.

The Spirit longs not just to empower, but also to guide us. That guidance has at least two parts. The Spirit desires to illuminate Scripture so our thinking is more thoroughly biblical. The Spirit also seeks to guide us day by day in our personal lives and in the work of the church.

The Spirit never contradicts God's revealed Word. Jesus promised that "the Counselor, the Holy Spirit, whom the Father will send in my name, will teach you all things and will remind you of everything I have said to you" (John 14:26). The Spirit illuminates our minds so we can more accurately grasp what Jesus and the Scriptures teach. Some people misunderstand the Spirit's role, claim special divine revelation, and abandon biblical authority. At its worst, a

confused emphasis on the Spirit's special personal reve-
lations to them become just a charismatic version of post-
modern, individualistic subjectivism. That leads to disaster and heresy. What the Spirit longs to do, however, is help
us become more thoroughly biblical in our thinking.

The Spirit also wants to prompt and direct us day by day.
The biblical God is not a deist. Deists see God as a cosmic
clockmaker who designed a marvelously complex machine
that now runs on its own. In short, God never intervenes
miraculously in the world today. Deists think God would
be an incompetent clockmaker if he had to keep interfering to get his technology right.

Some Christians today are deists. Even some evangelicals who defend miracles in the Bible slip into deism when
they talk about the present.[10] But the picture of God the
Holy Spirit in the Book of Acts suggests a powerfully present God who freely works signs and wonders and provides
special guidance for the church from day to day.

Luke's account of Paul's first missionary journey throbs
with the directing, guiding presence of the Holy Spirit.
"While they were worshiping the Lord and fasting, the Holy
Spirit said, 'Set apart for me Barnabas and Saul for the work
to which I have called them.' So after they had fasted and
prayed, they placed their hands on them and sent them off.
The two of them, sent on their way by the Holy Spirit, went
down to Seleucia and sailed from there to Cyprus" (Acts
13:2–4). Later, on his second missionary trip, Paul wanted to go into Bithynia, but "the Spirit of Jesus would not
allow them to" (Acts 16:7). Instead, the Spirit sent them to
Europe.

I want that kind of daily guidance in my life and work.
I believe God wants Evangelicals for Social Action (which
I serve as president) to be just as eager and sensitive to the
direction of the Holy Spirit as was Paul as he began his
missionary travels. I think the Spirit wants to guide every
Christian, every congregation, every Christian organiza-

tion and denomination—if we will truly listen and constantly invite the Spirit's prompting.

That does not mean we should not also think and strategize. It does not mean we despise long-range planning or even effective advertising. God has blessed us with rational minds and wants us to use them. Paul combines using the mind and depending on the Spirit in a striking passage in 1 Corinthians 14. He cautions against speaking in tongues unless there is interpretation. "For if I pray in a tongue, my spirit prays, but my mind is unfruitful. So what shall I do? I will pray with my spirit, but I will also pray with my mind; I will sing with my spirit, but I will also sing with my mind" (1 Cor. 14:14–15). Enjoying the fullness of the Spirit does not mean abandoning careful thought.

We must, of course, submit our minds unconditionally to the Lord. But that does not mean we stop thinking. Spirit-filled persons who know Christ's dawning kingdom begins the renewal of creation should think and strategize to the full. They should also, with equal zeal, pray without ceasing and seek the Spirit's guidance every moment.

Sometimes the Spirit intervenes miraculously to guide and direct. Sometimes not. But for the sovereign Creator, all things work together for good. We need not know what is miracle and what is providence. The relationship between nature and grace will always remain a mystery in this life.

It is Satan's trick, not the Creator's intention, when Christians think they must choose between prayer and thought, unconditional dependence on the Holy Spirit and careful, sophisticated planning. We should immerse our strategizing in intercession and combine our prayer with analysis. Both, after all, were the ideas of the Creator who is also the Spirit.

Our marketing technologies and fund-raising methods tempt us to become deists and forget the Spirit. How many Christian congregations and Christian organizations do you know that pray and fast for the guidance of the Spirit the way the early church did? And then at the same time plan and strategize with equal care? Some do one, some do the other. Only a very few do both. I wonder what God would do if we enthusiastically embraced both. Perhaps the story of Kriengsak Chareonwongsak suggests the answer.

I must confess that the Christian board meetings I attend and the Christian organizations I know best are much better in their theology of the Spirit than in their practical experience of the Spirit. I long for a more biblical balance. I can hardly wait to see what God would do through a people whose minds were razor-sharp and whose total being was unconditionally open to the Spirit.

Some years ago, as I was asking God to show me whether I should devote a large amount of time to lead Evangelicals for Social Action, I wrote a prayer. I share it here to renew my pledge to submit my life unconditionally to God and live by the divine power that the Spirit gives as we pray. I invite you to make it your prayer.

Father, in the morning of this new day, I joyfully and gratefully submit every fiber of my being to you and your will. I surrender every corner of my life, every ounce of personal ambition, striving, and longing to you and your kingdom. By your grace, I ask for that purity of heart that wills only one thing—your will and glory.

Lord Jesus, in the morning of this new day, I ask for the grace to make every decision and perform every single act according to the values of your kingdom, according to the model you lived and taught.

And, blessed Holy Spirit, in the morning of this new day, I implore you to shower upon me the fullness of your fruits, gifts, and power. Please intercede for me with groans too deep for human utterance so that all this day I may live and act for the honor and glory of the God whom I love and adore, Father, Son, and Holy Spirit. Amen.

Part 2

THE CHURCH

5

A LITTLE PICTURE
OF HEAVEN

Characteristic Five

Genuine Christians strive to make the church a little picture of what heaven will be like

In the last book of the Bible, John paints a glorious picture of heaven. All tears, hunger, violence, and prejudice have fled. Standing around the throne and praising God are "a great multitude that no one could count, from every nation, tribe, people and language" (Rev. 7:9). A vast multiracial assembly from every nation on earth stands united in love to worship their one Savior.

By contrast, take a quick look around planet earth. Racial prejudice and ethnic hostility simmer everywhere, only to explode suddenly in deadly destruction. While classes compete, the poorest starve, and the rich seek fulfillment in ever greater material abundance. Ugly hatreds, rooted as they are in distorted ideas about race, wealth, and gender, rend and destroy the human family.

Two pictures: one of a reconciled humanity in heaven; the other of a warring chaos on earth.

Now ponder the churches you know. Are they more like the first picture or the second?

There is no simple answer. We all know striking examples of both. But the familiar instances of broken churches abound and seem particularly ghastly. Protestants and Catholics have murdered each other for decades in Northern Ireland. Serbian Orthodox and Croatian Catholics rape and kill each other in senseless genocide. In the United States, eleven o'clock Sunday morning is still the most racially segregated hour of the week. Most congregations divide, just like society, along lines of race and class.

That kind of church has no credibility. That kind of church misunderstands the gospel. That kind of church has no power to transform society.

African-American evangelist Tom Skinner was right: God wants the church to be a little picture of what heaven will be like. Why? Because breaking down sinful dividing walls is at the core of the gospel. Because believing women and men of every race, tribe, and income are one body in Christ. Because the gospel is not only forgiveness, it is the Good News of the dawning kingdom. And because Jesus prayed for a visible, loving unity among his disciples so striking that it would convince the world that he came from the Father.

The worst racial prejudice of the ancient world was between Jews and Gentiles, who were separated by an ugly "dividing wall of hostility." But Paul dared to claim that the gospel "put to death their hostility" (Eph. 2:16). How? Because both Jews and Gentiles stand together at the foot of the cross, reconciled to God in exactly the same way, both now receiving unconditional forgiveness as they cling to Christ. And since they are reconciled to God, they must also be reconciled to each other, which, in fact, is exactly what God intended. His "purpose was to create in himself one new man out of the two, thus making peace, and in this one body to reconcile both of them to God through the cross, by which he put to death their hostility" (Eph. 2:15-16).

God's purpose in salvation includes racial reconciliation. Genuine reconciliation with God is inseparable from reconciliation with believers from other races.

Furthermore, the new, reconciled multiracial body of believers is part of the gospel. After Paul's amazing words in Ephesians 2 about how Christ ends racial division, he proceeds to talk about the mystery of the gospel that he preaches (Eph. 3:3-4, 7). What is this mystery? "This mystery is that through the gospel the Gentiles are heirs together with Israel, members together of one body" (v. 6). One part of the Good News we preach is the astounding fact that right now in the power of the Holy Spirit there is a new redeemed community where racial and ethnic hostilities are disappearing.

Ultimately, racism in the church is a denial of the gospel. It is a heretical, disobedient rejection of God's purpose in Christ, which is why Paul publicly rebuked Peter for racial bias, condemning Peter for "not acting in line with the truth of the gospel" (Gal. 2:14). Racial reconciliation in the church is a visible demonstration of the gospel.

Nor does the gospel's power to tear down hostile walls end with the problem of racism, for Paul repeatedly boasted of the way Christ overcame other prejudices and divisions in the ancient world. Masters oppressed slaves. Men despised women. Educated, cultural "Greeks" scorned less fortunate "barbarians." But Christ died for all. Women, slaves, barbarians, and Gentiles were justified freely through Christ, just as Jewish men were. Paul wrote that where there is only one baptism, one Spirit, one body, "there is no Greek or Jew, circumcised or uncircumcised, barbarian, Scythian, slave or free, but Christ is all, and is in all" (Col. 3:11).

Paul never tired of underscoring the astonishing implications of the theological truth that all believers are one body in Christ. Like the parts of the human body, all Christians have dignity in that one body and lovingly serve the body's other members (1 Cor. 12). "If one part suffers, every part suffers with it; if one part is honored, every part rejoices with it" (v. 26).

Nor was the early church talking about some fuzzy, abstract, invisible unity. Being one in Christ meant mutual accountability and responsibility for each other's spiritual growth (Gal. 6:1–2). It also meant sweeping economic sharing. At Jerusalem, believers with resources shared so generously "as [any] had need" that "there were no needy persons among them" (Acts 2:45; 4:34). Paul considered this economic fellowship so important that he spent years organizing an intercontinental offering. Greek-speaking European believers shared sacrificially with poor Aramaic-speaking Asians in Jerusalem. Paul considered that economic sharing to be a visible demonstration of the unity of Christ's one worldwide, multiracial body. In this sense, the New Testament is simply the continuation of a theme that runs throughout the Old Testament as well, that central to God's plan of salvation is a new redeemed people living very differently from the world. And one striking mark of their difference is astonishing economic sharing among God's people.[1]

An amazing story from the fourth century underlines the power of this kind of sharing. Fifty years after Constantine ended the Roman Empire's persecution of Christians, a hostile pagan emperor came to power. For a few short years, Julian the Apostate tried to restore paganism and stamp out Christianity, but he failed—in part because his pagan subjects, unlike the Christians, refused to share with the poor. Julian grudgingly admitted to a fellow pagan "that the godless Galileans [Christians] feed not only their poor but ours also."[2]

Jesus' explicit teaching is the most important reason why the church should be a little picture of what heaven will be like. Anybody who claims to be a Christian should take Jesus' definition of the gospel very seriously. Virtually every time Jesus used the word *gospel,* he defined it as the Good News of the kingdom (Mark 1:14–15 and Luke 4:43, for example).[3]

Why is that important? Jesus' definition prevents us from reducing the gospel to a cheap one-way ticket to heaven. Because the gospel most assuredly includes unmerited forgiveness, we can stand before God without fear. Because the New Testament explicitly teaches that it is more than that, we rightly expect Christians to live very differently from the world.

When Jesus announced the gospel of the kingdom, he meant that the Messiah and his kingdom, which had long before been promised by the prophets, was actually arriving. The prophets had promised that the Messiah would bring both sweeping forgiveness and a redeemed community. In the Messianic time, there would be peace, justice for the poor, and wholeness (Isa. 9:1–6; 11:1–9; Jer. 31:31–34).

All that happened when Jesus came. He astonished prostitutes and tax collectors and prodigal sons and daughters with his unconditional forgiveness. Then he gently told them to go and sin no more. He challenged society's violence, men's disrespect for women, and rich people's neglect of the poor and marginalized. Urging these forgiven sinners to live as he did, he offered this new redeemed community as a visible sign of the dawning messianic kingdom. In spite of failure, the early church followed in his steps. That is why Paul could say that the new multiethnic church was part of the gospel he preached.

Jesus' final prayer is probably the most astonishing statement about the importance of our need to mirror the love of heaven. Earlier, Jesus had promised that if his disciples loved each other the way he loved them, then "everyone will know that you are my disciples" (John 13:34–36 NRSV). Then, as recorded in John 17, he actually prays that our love and unity will be so visible and striking that it will convince a watching world that he did indeed come from the Father: "May they be brought to complete unity to let the world know that you sent me" (vv. 20–23).

Jesus must weep when he sees how his body today conforms to racial prejudice, nationalistic arrogance, sexual discrimination, and class bias. He pleads with us to let the Holy Spirit sweep through our prejudice and create one new body in which there is neither black nor white, male nor female, rich nor poor. He longs for us to become a little picture of what heaven will be like.

To put it more precisely and more biblically: God wants the church to be a preliminary picture of the kingdom that Christ will bring. For me, both statements mean the same thing. But Greek philosophy has misled some Christians into thinking of heaven as some immaterial world of invisible souls almost totally unrelated to the world we know. That is not the biblical perspective. Romans 8 teaches that God will purge this groaning creation of evil and decay on the day of Christ's return (vv. 19–22). God intends to purge sin so that "the glory and honor of the nations will be brought" into the new Jerusalem (Rev. 21:26). Resurrected bodily from the dead, you and I will sing and dance forever in a renewed creation free of injustice, oppression, and death. When Christ returns, I expect to go hiking in the Himalayas and sailing on the Mediterranean with Paul and a multiracial crew of men and women from every nation and class. It is for that glorious celebration that the church is now preparing.

If we grasp the glorious biblical vision of the church as a transformed, redeemed community, things will change.

We will refuse to accept the sinful walls of hostility that divide and ravage the fallen world. By God's grace, your congregation and mine will become little pictures of what heaven will be like.

The implications are clear and momentous. Christ calls us to end the scandal of racism in his body. Christ summons his wealthy followers to share with poor sisters and brothers in the way the first Christians did. Christ pleads with Christian men to affirm the dignity and equality of women in the way he did. Christ urges each of us to treasure our Christian identity more than our nationality.

I don't pretend that this is easy. I have struggled with interracial friendships for years only to find some of them dissolve in mistrust and separation. The history of white European arrogance and oppression has been long and destructive. And because of that, the fear, mistrust, even hatred in the hearts of non-whites, is paralyzing. The wounds—and the guilt—are deep. I once heard a prominent Third World evangelical, who has worked with Christians on all continents, confess that there are only three white men in the world that he really trusts.

Christian women still do not have equal respect and opportunity in the church. Sexual abuse is painfully widespread in Christian homes.

The gap between rich and poor continues to widen. In 1960, the richest 20 percent of the world's countries had thirty times more income than the poorest 20 percent.[4] By 1990, the richest 20 percent had 60 times more! Since Christians own two-thirds of the world's wealth, the majority of that top 20 percent were "Christians." While we get richer, one billion desperately poor people live at the edge of survival. Millions starve every year. Tens of millions of these desperate people are brothers and sisters in Christ. That we tolerate their anguish is a sinful rending of Christ's one body.

No matter what it costs, the scandal of Christians killing Christians must cease. It is a heretical denial of the biblical gospel when Serbian Christians, Rwandan Christians, American Christians, or Russian Christians place a higher value on their ethnic or national identity than on their unity in Christ.

How can more congregations truly become more faithful pictures of heaven?

First, *we must pray for revival.* Only God can make that happen. Without a mighty movement of God's Spirit, it is impossible. The new movements of prayer in the church today are a strong sign of hope. We must plead with God to renew and transform us and our churches.

Second, *we need a more biblical theology of the church.* Biblical churches are visible signs of Christ's dawning kingdom, not comfortable clubs of conformity to the world. We need to recover the clear biblical distinction between the church and the world. That does not mean physical separation from non-Christians. But it does mean separation from their sin.

"What does a believer have in common with an unbeliever? . . . 'Therefore come out from them and be separate,' says the Lord. . . . Let us purify ourselves from everything that contaminates body and spirit, perfecting holiness out of reverence for God" (2 Cor. 6:15–7:1).

People often misunderstand Jesus' parable of the wheat and the weeds to justify broadly inclusive churches that never dare to challenge sin in their midst. Jesus tells the story of a man who sowed wheat in the field and then discovered that an enemy had secretly planted weeds all through the wheat. Jesus said no to those who wanted immediately to run and pull up all the weeds. "Let both grow together until the harvest," Jesus directed.

Does that mean that church discipline is wrong? Is it in the church that weeds and wheat should grow together? Not at all! Jesus himself explains the parable: "The field is the world and . . . the harvest is the end of the age" (Matt. 13:37–39). This parable affirms religious freedom and toleration in society rather than Christian acceptance of open sin in the church. The parable in no way contradicts Jesus' explicit command in Matthew 18:15–19 to exercise church discipline and remove from the body of believers those who persist in open sin. The church will renew its strength only if we recover the New Testament understanding of the church as a committed body of believers living like Christ rather than the world.

Third, *we need new structures in the local congregation and in the broader body.* I wish every Christian would be in a small group that meets weekly to worship, pray, and hold each other accountable. I am convinced that the sinful pressures of the larger society are so strong that it is nearly impossible to follow Jesus without close, regular Christian fellowship. In our crazy society, it is *very hard* to resist advertisers' alluring materialism and Hollywood's seductive sexual nonsense. We need the daily prayer, regular encouragement, and honest challenge of trusted sisters and brothers to live like Jesus.

John Wesley discovered the power of small groups in the early years of Methodism. Weekly, they would meet together for prayer, singing, and confession. The leaders asked tough questions! "Do you desire to be told all your faults? . . . What known sin have you committed since our last meeting?"[5] "Watching over one another in love" was Wesley's wonderful phrase for this mutual accountability.

That kind of small group structure was at the heart of Methodism for one hundred years. During those same years, Methodism spread around the world. It also became the largest denomination in the United States.

An insignificant, slightly embarrassing personal story underlines the power of small groups. While writing this book, I became uneasy about a snap decision I had made a couple months earlier at my favorite thrift store. I discovered a lovely winter coat with a white price tag marked $25.00. I wasn't certain, but I thought that all items with that color tag were going at half price that day. When I got to the cash register, I held up the ticket and asked if it was 50 percent off. The clerk said no, but then misread the $25.00 and punched in $2.50. I said nothing.

But I felt uneasy as I drove home and showed Arbutus the coat. With some frequency, in the following weeks, the incident came to mind during my private devotions. Finally, I decided I would share the story with our small group. To my (slight) annoyance, they laughed hilariously—and then insisted that I take the coat back. I agreed and told them to hold me accountable at our next meeting. And take it back I did—the afternoon before our small group met again. Would I have returned the coat if no one else knew about the clerk's error?

People who have learned over months and years to love and trust each other can help us follow Jesus in far more momentous things. They are a great place to discuss family budgets, charitable donations, the joys and struggles of parenting and marriage, the tough temptations over sex and money, and the big decisions about vocation. I am absolutely convinced that God will dramatically transform any local congregation that develops well-led small groups that most members attend regularly for a significant length of time. Small groups are one of the best structures for conquering individualism, defying surrounding society, and watching over one another in love.

We also need new ways to demonstrate Christian love for other Christians beyond the local congregation. Recently, I have visited a number of the larger congregations in Philadelphia and its suburbs. It was deeply painful to see so starkly how thoroughly the body of Christ is still divided along racial lines. If the new multiracial body of believers is an inseparable part of the biblical gospel, then this scandal must end. That does not mean that every congregation must have an equal number of people from all races and languages and cultures. It does mean, however, that unless we are to continue in open rebellion against the gospel, we must discover *regular, visible* ways to demonstrate to ourselves and the world that black and white believers, inner-city and suburban Christians, are truly one.

There are many ways to do that. Every church that is predominantly of one race or class should develop a long-term partnership–free of paternalism–with a different kind of church. Once a quarter, all the Christians in an area could rent the largest sports stadiums and convention centers for glorious multicultural Christian celebrations. Quarterly celebrations like this that continued over many years would change us.

At the national and international level, we also need to transcend lingering racism. It is wonderful news that in South Africa, the predominantly black Concerned Evangelicals and the largely white Evangelical Fellowship of South Africa are planning to merge. In the United States, the white National Association of Evangelicals and the National Black Evangelical Association held a reconciliation conference in early 1995 where merger was mentioned. How much better if black and white evangelicals in South Africa had made this move a few years before rather than a few years after the politicians ended apartheid. How much better if evangelicals in the United States had made their move three decades before rather than three decades after Martin Luther King Jr. and the black church led the costly struggle for civil rights. But even now both mergers–done with mutual respect and genuine partnership–would help make the church a little more like what heaven will be.

As an example, I believe the Memphis Miracle of 1994 gives hope that God is beginning to move in mighty new ways.[6] It was the culmination of several years of dialogue and confession, as prominent leaders from both black and white Pentecostal churches came together, and spontaneously, prominent leaders knelt in repentance to wash the feet of Christians from another race. The largely white Pentecostal Fellowship of North America voted itself out of existence. The next day a new, inclusive multiracial organization chaired by an African-American bishop was formed. A woman, Bishop Barbara Amos, also serves on the governing board.

At a time when society seems to be moving toward greater polarization, God is stirring the church to model oneness in Christ. It is a time to hope and dream.

I have a dream for my home town of Philadelphia. Philadelphia is typical of U.S. cities. Vast sections of the inner city are very poor and overwhelmingly black or Hispanic. Most middle-class whites and some middle-class blacks have moved to the suburbs–along with most of the good jobs and excellent schools. Here and there, like the Philadelphia neighborhood called Germantown where Arbutus and I live, are small interracial pockets. But the city and the suburbs–and the churches most of all–are largely segregated by race and class.

I dream that the Christians of greater Philadelphia would remember their oneness in Christ and decide to demonstrate it to themselves and to the world. I dream that they would resolve that it is a violation of the body of Christ to tolerate a situation where poor, inner-city people who love Jesus have inadequate schools, poor jobs, and wretched housing while suburban Christians enjoy good schools, jobs, and homes.

In my dream, Christians don't curse the darkness. They light candles–and change structures. Pastors and leading laity from all the churches join together to develop alternative schools and transform public education so every child has the opportunity to acquire a high-quality education. They volunteer time, supplies, and money so that Habitat for Humanity can help every interested family in the city build or renovate a home to call their own. Christian business leaders throughout the metropolitan area decide that there will be a job with a decent salary for every person who can and wants to work. Through a variety of new initiatives, both private and public, they transform city and suburbs.

At regular intervals, all the churches in the greater Philadelphia area rent Veteran's Stadium, the Civic Center, and the new Pennsylvania Convention Center to worship together in joyful multiracial festivals of Christian unity. Together they repent of racism and covenant never again to allow Satan to divide them by class or gender or race. Together, they pledge never to rest until every Christian—indeed every person—in the whole metropolis has the opportunity for a good education, a job to support a family, and a decent home in a safe neighborhood to enjoy God's gorgeous gift of life. Together they worship the risen Lord in multicultural celebrations of praise and proclamation. Together they tell the whole city that all their labor flows from gratitude to their Savior who died to reconcile them to God and each other. And together they invite all who have never met him to join them at the foot of the cross.

Our first goal would simply be for the church to be the church. We would, of course, offer help to non-Christians as well as Christians. We would seek to make government operate justly. But our first intention would only be to become the kind of church the New Testament describes. Our first goal would be to let God create within the entire Christian community of greater Philadelphia a little miniature of what heaven will be like.

Unlikely? Yes. Unbiblical? No. In fact, I cannot see how we can claim to understand what the New Testament says about the church unless Christians do something like this.

Impossible? Not at all. It would be costly, but no middle-class Christian would need to embrace poverty in order to help pay for it. In addition to what we now give to charity, the vast majority of us could contribute 10 percent of our time and 10 percent of our income without falling into poverty. That would be more than enough—even if only 20 percent of those who call themselves Christians joined in for a couple decades.

Does anyone doubt what our Lord would think?

And the watching world? They would be stunned. Doubtful at first, their questioning surprise would give way to quiet admiration. To be sure, some would find ways to criticize and undermine. Many, however, would join the crusade—and accept our Lord.

My dream does not end with Philadelphia. I imagine the vision spreading to every nation on earth. We could do the same thing on a global scale. Since "Christians" already possess two-thirds of the world's wealth, money would be no problem. The only question is whether we are ready to say good-bye to the world and live like Jesus. If we do, Christ will create astonishing foretastes of his coming kingdom all across our planet. The world will see and believe—and be changed.

6

LOVING BOTH
BODY AND SOUL

Characteristic Six

Genuine Christians love the whole person the way Jesus did

Cassandra was a frightened single mom on welfare in one of Chicago's poorest neighborhoods. When her doctor told her she was pregnant again, she agonized over the possibility of an abortion. Fortunately, her doctor worked at a Christian medical clinic and suggested that she talk to one of the pastors of the church connected with this holistic community center.

Cassandra expected a stern preacher to give her a fire-and-brimstone sermon. Instead she found a gentle friend. He listened, invited her to church, and told her about Jesus' love for her. When she accepted Christ a few weeks later, a new peace and joy began to flow through her life.

Her boyfriend, however, was suspicious. All her talk about Jesus and Pastor Grant made Showen jealous, but he could not deny that something beautiful was beginning to happen to his girlfriend. One Sunday, he decided to check things out for himself. After Pastor Grant's sermon, Showen too accepted Christ.

That was the easy part. It took Cassandra and Showen four more years of struggle to learn what it really means to follow Christ. "I had accepted Christ into my heart," Showen reports, "but I had not made him Lord of my life." Lovingly, patiently, Paul Grant and his wife Du Rhonda walked and prayed with Cassandra and Showen, who slowly grew in Christ until they decided to marry—the first Christian marriage in either of their immediate families. They asked God to use their marriage as a witness to their relatives about the goodness of Christ-centered marriage. God has answered their prayer. Several of Showen's close relatives have also become Christians.

Showen and Cassandra are not on welfare today. Cassandra works full time at Circle Urban Ministries (CUM), a multimillion-dollar-a-year complex of programs in remedial education, recreation, health services, job training, and small business development. Showen is now the general manager of CUM's most successful small business. On-the-job training developed Showen's natural gifts. In 1993, the company he manages employed twelve people full time and cleared a net profit of fifty thousand dollars.

God dramatically transformed Showen and Cassandra Franklin. How? Through Christians at this wonderful church and community center sharing the whole gospel with them and then walking arm-in-arm as God transformed them into whole persons.[1]

I wonder what would have happened if Cassandra and Showen had wandered into a typical church. Many theologically liberal congregations would have gladly given them food baskets, health care, and job training. Tragically, however, they would probably never have gotten around to telling them that they could have a personal relationship with the Savior who longs to change their hearts and habits. Many theologically conservative churches would have told them about Christ, but they might never have offered a doctor or a job, because that smacks of the "social gospel."

But Showen and Cassandra needed both in order to experience the wholeness God wants them to enjoy. Fortunately, God led them to Rock Church and Circle Urban Ministries, where faithful Christians care about the body and the soul—together. Like Jesus, they care about the whole person. The result for Showen and Cassandra was sweeping, lasting transformation that continues to ripple through a large extended family. Caring for the whole person, like Jesus, works miracles. Lopsided Christianity cannot.

This story points to one of the most important reasons for the weakness of the modern church. The roots of the problem are complex, but at the beginning of the twentieth century, one branch of Christianity—the "social gospel" branch—realized the need to focus on social action. At the same time, another large group—the evangelicals—felt called to focus on evangelism. For decades they criticized each other. Social gospel people claimed that Jesus and the rest of the Bible compel us to care about the physical needs of people. And they were right. Evangelical folk insisted that according to Jesus and the Scriptures, nothing is as important as a living relationship with God in Christ. And they too were right. Tragically, foolishly, each side used the other side's sinful neglect of one half of Christian mission to justify their own stubborn neglect of the other half. The result has been lopsided, ineffective churches.

How could people who confess Jesus as both true God and true man reject Jesus' example? How could people who worship Christ as the Eternal Word become flesh ignore his perfect combination of word and deed?

The Church

Jesus' tender concern for the whole person—soul and body—is clear in every Gospel. He preached and he healed. He satisfied sick hearts and sick bodies. Matthew says it pointedly: "Jesus went through all the towns and villages, teaching in their synagogues, preaching the good news of the kingdom and healing every disease and sickness" (Matt. 9:35).

Why? Because he loved people—whole people. Again and again, the Gospels say Jesus healed people because he had compassion for them (Matt. 14:14; 15:32; 20:34; Mark 1:41). His tender concern for the widow who had just lost her son still moves us across twenty centuries: "When the Lord saw her, his heart went out to her, and he said, 'Don't cry'" (Luke 7:13). Jesus raised the boy because his heart ached for this lonely, weeping widow.

The Gospels clearly demonstrate that Jesus spent a lot of time healing physical brokenness. But it was not because he thought life here on earth was the most important thing. Explicitly, pointedly, Jesus taught that even if one gained absolutely everything in this world, it would not be worth losing one's relationship with God (Mark 8:34–38). The Creator designed us to live forever with him. Absolutely nothing in the world—not even everything in the world!—is worth jeopardizing that relationship.

Tragically, Christians often distort this important teaching. Some Christians conclude from Mark 8:34–38 that evangelism is the only thing that really matters. Saving souls is our central concern. Healing sick bodies and broken societies is unimportant.

Jesus never said that. His actions prove exactly the opposite. Jesus could have spent all of his time preaching and urging people to repent. After all, he knew better than anybody else how important it is to come to personal faith in the living God. But a careful look at the Gospels shows that Jesus spent about as much time ministering to people's physical needs as he did preaching. If Jesus is truly God

90

in the flesh, then he is our perfect model. Since he cared for the whole person, so should we. If we don't, we disobey the One we worship.

Jesus cared about whole persons because he was the Creator. He knew we have been created, not merely as bodies and not merely as souls. Every person is a "body-soul-in-community."[2]

Any view that reduces us primarily or exclusively to mere bodies or mere souls is simply unbiblical. Since we are not merely material beings, nothing in the material world can finally satisfy us. Material wealth, sex, political power are all finally inadequate. We are made for a relationship with God, and we are invited to live forever in God's presence. Therefore, any solution to the human problem that focuses primarily on economic development or structural change via politics is bound to fail.

On the other hand, our bodies are not a mere accident. The Creator made us body-soul unities. Even when Paul longed to leave the body and be with the Lord, he insisted that God's final plan for us is *bodily* resurrection–that wholeness of body-soul unity intended by the Creator (2 Cor. 5:1–4; 1 Cor. 15:35–44). If the body is so good that the Creator became flesh, rose bodily, and promises to restore the whole created order including our bodies, then any approach to human need that ignores or neglects physical needs is flatly heretical.

Black evangelist/social activist John Perkins underlines this point. As he worked in the midst of white racism, whites often said, "John, I love your soul." They wanted to lead him to Christ without struggling against racial and economic oppression. Perkins's answer is profoundly biblical: "My soul is in a black body. If you really want to get to my soul, you're first going to have to deal with this body."[3]

Jesus' teaching and example and the Bible's view of persons are just two of many biblical reasons why genuine Christians refuse to spend all their time and energy on evangelism. As we shall see in chapter nine, the God of the Bible has a special concern for the poor and weak, and he commands his people to share his concern. Furthermore, Christ is Lord of all of life, including economics and politics (see chapter eight). In chapter five, which discussed the church, we saw how being one in Christ means caring about the physical and spiritual needs of other believers. And when Christ returns, believers will be resurrected bodily, the groaning creation will be restored to wholeness, and the glory of the nations will enter the new Jerusalem. If the Bible is true, then the physical world, human life, and history matter a lot to God.

People are made to live on this good earth and enjoy its wonders for "three score years and ten." The splendor of soaring Rockies, the ecstasy of a couple in love, and the beauty of Mozart and Michaelangelo are all astounding gifts from a boundless, loving Creator. But they are not the Creator. They are rings from our Beloved, not the Beloved himself.

But we are also made to live and reign forever with the risen Lord in a restored world. Life then will be different from history as we now experience it. Nothing in the world we now enjoy is worth as much as a saving relationship with Christ who gives eternal life. If we keep our hearts fixed on the Divine Lover as we treasure and delight in his gorgeous gifts, we will be able to keep a biblical balance between evangelism and social transformation.

What a tragedy that some Christians today are embarrassed to tell their friends about this wonderful Savior. What a tragedy that some Christians are so preoccupied with correcting injustice and restoring the environment that they never find time to tell dying persons that God invites them to eternal joy in the divine embrace.

Nothing is more important for every Christian today than sharing Jesus with those who do not yet know him. Faithful Christians nurture a passion for evangelism at the center of their prayers and action.

We evangelize because of God's astounding love. God so loved the world that he gave his only Son so that all who believe will not perish (John 3:16). If we have been sought and embraced by transforming love, how can we fail to lead others to that same embrace?

We share the gospel because we understand the uniqueness of Christ. The Galilean champion of marginalized women, lepers, and beggars was the Eternal Word in whom God was pleased to have all his fullness dwell (Col. 1:19). If we believe the church's central confession that the Creator of the galaxies once trod the dusty paths of our little planet to bring us salvation, how can we fail to tell others that long ago in Palestine God became flesh for us?

We tell others about the Savior because Jesus is the only way to salvation. With Peter, we confess that "there is salvation in no one else, for there is no other name under heaven given among mortals by which we must be saved" (Acts 4:12 NRSV). If we know he is the only way, how can we neglect to tell those who have not heard?

We proclaim the gospel in submission to his last command. Gladly, obediently, we go into every nation on earth inviting all people everywhere to become disciples, receive baptism, and obey all that Christ taught (Matt. 28:19–20). If we know who he is, dare we disobey his last command?

We spread the Good News because Jesus is the best gift we have to offer. We know that there is absolutely nothing we could share with others that would bring them anywhere nearly as much joy and blessing as a living knowledge of our Lord. Can we love our neighbors and not share our best treasure?

We also announce the gospel because we know people are lost, both now and forever, without Jesus Christ. Knowing that "all have sinned and fall short of the glory of God" (Rom. 3:23), knowing that some people will someday hear Jesus' terrifying words, "depart from me, you who are cursed, into the eternal fire" (Matt. 25:41), we evangelize with a holy urgency. If we believe Jesus' warning, how can we fail to shout in fear and trembling: Please dear son, daughter, neighbor, turn from the way of death to your loving Savior who seeks you with arms outstretched!

We invite people to Christ because in Jesus' life, death, and resurrection, God has drawn back the curtain and offered us a little glimpse of the future. We know it is God's good pleasure that eventually the kingdoms of this world will become the kingdom of our Lord (Rev. 11:15) and that even the groaning creation will be healed at Christ's return. If we understand God's grand design, how can we not eagerly invite people to enjoy its splendor?

Finally, we share the gospel so that the whole world may be full of God's glory. Paul longed for the day when every tongue would "confess that Jesus Christ is Lord, to the glory of God the Father" (Phil. 2:11). Having tasted the sweet, awesome splendor of God's glory, will we not eagerly seek to spread it throughout the universe?

Our broken world needs nothing as much as the gospel. But it must be the biblical gospel, not some watered down, lopsided version. Faithful Christians gladly embrace both evangelism and social concern. Biblical faith demands it. Jesus modeled it. And it works!

We saw how Rock/Circle's loving combination of word and deed radically transformed the lives of Showen and Cassandra Franklin. But their story is not an accident or an isolated incident. Hundreds and hundreds of people have come to faith in Christ in the last ten years through the church and community center at Rock/Circle.

The same thing is happening in scores of other holistic ministries that (like Rock/Circle) are part of the Christian Community Development Association. Consider, for example, my friend Bishop Dickie Robbins, who pastors a church in one of the poorest neighborhoods in one of the poorest cities in the country.

I first met Bishop Robbins when he took my class on holistic ministry. I soon discovered that he was already practicing what I was preaching about linking evangelism and social action. Thirty percent of the 230 members at Life in Christ Cathedral of Faith in Chester, Pennsylvania, have come to the church through its holistic ministry to people hooked on drugs and alcohol. In fact, other churches sometimes refer to this congregation as "the little drug church on Third Street." In their Drug Free Ministry–and the many other social ministries run by this small congregation–evangelism is central. And people are transformed.

When David Scott first got to know Bishop Robbins, his life was a disaster. David had been on drugs for twenty-three years and was facing a likely eight-to-fifteen-year prison term. Bishop Robbins led him to personal faith in Christ and told him to marry the woman he was living with. Fortunately, David received eleven months on work release instead of time in jail and was able to work every day with Bishop Robbins. The Holy Spirit used Robbins's intense, extended discipleship program to work wonders. Today Elder Scott and his wife, Carol, are among Bishop Robbins's most important leaders. David oversees all the church's social ministries–and still finds time to serve on a board at Crozier Hospital along with one of the county judges.

Life in Christ's ministries are changing their community. Their Love in Feeding Everyone (LIFE) ministry provides meals for 150 people each week. Drug Free Ministry serves at least sixty people a week. Generation of Destiny tutors and mentors teenagers so they never get hooked on drugs. Eagle's Nest Academy makes quality education available for about 130 kids, many from poor families, from grades K through 11. (The public school system is ranked last out of 501 districts in the state!) Each ministry will have its own 501(c)3 status, but Bishop Robbins chairs each board to make sure it reflects the church's holistic vision.

From the beginning, Bishop Robbins was determined to build a church that would transform people and the surrounding community. He told the local newspaper that he came to do "more than just set up another church." He planned to "build a ministry." In one of his powerful sermons, he compares churches to car repair shops. There are two types: "Both have the same equipment, but one produces fixed cars and one doesn't." Broken people come into Bishop Robbins's repair shop—and come out transformed. "The way to determine how effective a ministry is is to see how the people come out, not how they come in."

Gerald Pierce came in hurting. When Dickie Robbins returned to his hometown of Chester, he heard reports that his former classmate (and a gifted musician) was using drugs—even while serving as a church musician. His marriage was on the rocks and he had lost his kids. Bishop Robbins invited Gerald to join him. Robbins said he could not pay much money, but he promised tough discipling! Gerald agreed.

Today Elder Pierce leads the church's extensive program in music and fine arts: drama, praise dance, mime, step, and choirs. He just released an album called "Let It Rain," which he wrote and produced. "The devil thought he had destroyed Gerald," Bishop Robbins says, "but God has turned him around. Through his music and ministry, people are getting saved all over."

God has only begun to work wonders at Life in Christ Cathedral of Faith. The church has plans for ministries in economic development, prison ministry, and fine arts evangelism. But Bishop Robbins believes that it is crucial to wait until leaders have been trained. So he is investing in a training program in which each leader trains another leader. The congregation's 230 members are committed. Before you can join the church, you have to complete a ten-week class for new members—and also sign up to work in at least one church ministry. This congregation is poised for explosive growth.

That is good news. It is even better news that holistic ministries like Life in Christ Cathedral of Faith in Chester and Rock/Circle in Chicago are flourishing all around the world. Vinay and Colleen Samuel's similar programs in a desperately poor neighborhood in India serve fifty thousand people and regularly lead persons to Christ. Ichthus Fellowship, with its emphasis on words, works, and wonders among the poor of London, has grown from fourteen people to over two thousand in twenty years. I know of dozens of mature ministries serving the whole person all around the world. I have told some of the best stories in *Cup of Water, Bread of Life.* In the United States alone, the Christian Community Development Association has several hundred ministries seeking to develop in their local communities the kinds of holistic programs working so successfully at places like Rock/Circle.

There is good reason to think that the tragic separation of evangelism and social transformation is coming to an end. At its international congress in Manila in 1989, the Lausanne Committee for World Evangelization insisted that "good news and good works are inseparable."[4] Evangelicals who had formerly majored almost exclusively on evangelism are now increasingly also doing social ministry. Other Christians who had been hesitant about evangelism have reaffirmed their commitment to spread the gospel.

Think of the phenomenal growth of evangelical social ministries in the last few decades. World Vision exploded from a tiny ministry to Korean orphans to vast ministries in one hundred countries with an annual budget of $340 million (1994). Many other ministries like Compassion, World Relief, and World Concern raise tens of millions of dollars each year to feed the hungry and empower the poor.

Nor is it just traditional evangelical groups that are promoting evangelism. The worldwide Anglican communion designated the 1990s the "Decade of Evangelism." Pope John Paul II named 1990–2000 the "Universal Decade of Evangelism." His recent encyclicals *Redemptoris Missios* and *Ad Gentes* are a ringing plea for renewed attention to sharing the gospel with those who do not know Christ. "The poor are hungry for God, not just for bread and freedom."[5]

As the next two decades unfold, we could enjoy a better marriage of word and deed than at any time in the previous one hundred years. There are hundreds of mature holistic models like Rock/Circle and Life in Christ where evangelism and social concern walk hand in hand, transforming broken people and desperate neighborhoods. Their biblical balance and obvious success is inspiring thousands of newer ministers to imitate them as they have imitated Christ. We should pray and expect that God will raise up tens of thousands of ministries like Rock/Circle all around the world. In fact, would not a million please Jesus even more?

That's how I dream about the twenty-first century. I hope for a time when vast numbers of local churches have caught Jesus' vision of love for the whole person. I see thousands of Christian colleges, Bible schools, and seminaries all around the world captured by Jesus' model, sending out tens of thousands of skilled, enthusiastic leaders every year to pastor biblically balanced churches. I imagine scores of books, Sunday school lessons, and seminars training the laity to combine evangelism and social passion.

I dream of the day when the congregation that neglects evangelism or justice is the exception rather than the rule. I long for the time when most Christians are in congregations where each month they experience the joy of hearing about new people who have just begun to taste the goodness of salvation. I yearn for the day when most Christians are in congregations that walk with the needy, say no to all forms of prejudice, and reach out to heal broken communities.

I long for the day when the church truly obeys Jesus' last command: "As the Father has sent me, I am sending you" (John 20:21). If even a substantial minority in the church ever dares to do it his way, strongholds of Satan will fall, the angels will rejoice, and the world will be renewed.

And more and more desperate people like Juan de Jesús will find astounding peace in Christ.[6] In 1990, Juan was a bitter old drug addict dying of AIDS. In fact when Juan learned he had AIDS, he was so furious that he purposely infected about 2000 needles and syringes with his blood before selling them to drug users. Hundreds got AIDS. How then, five years later at Juan's funeral, could his pastor say that Juan was the best example of the power of God to change a person that he had ever seen?

Life as a young Puerto Rican in New York City was rough. His drug-abusing father and uncle taught him to use drugs and live off the prostitutes he conned as a fast-talking pimp. For years he lived in the fast lane. By the spring of 1991, however, he was hospitalized with an advanced case of AIDS. Each day he got worse. His doctor predicted that he would not see another birthday. Juan tried to commit suicide but the noose (of oxygen tubing) broke.

There was just one ray of hope as Juan lay dying. One Christian visitor frequently visited the hospital, sitting quietly at his bedside, talking to him, and asking how he could help. He helped him drink his juice and bought him some socks. Finally angry Juan was ready to listen as this visitor told him about God's love. One night soon after, Juan cried out: "Jesus, if you're really God, let me know you before I die."

Slowly he began to improve. His friend made plans to find him a home after he left the hospital. But the hospital gave Juan his valuables about an hour before his scheduled departure. Juan left by himself and promptly spent his money on drugs. Despair flooded back into his life.

Not long after, Juan again contemplated suicide as he sat alone and desperate in a park. Just then a young man came walking toward him. Juan's first thought was to do what he had so often done in the past–knock him down with his brass knuckles and rob him. But the young man walked right up and announced: "Jesus loves you. My dad used to be an addict like you, and Jesus helped him stop."

Still Juan hesitated. Should he smack him? Juan wavered. Then, hesitantly he consented to go with the young man. Juan found a church full of love, joy, and exuberance. He came to faith in Christ and gladly accepted the church's offer to find him a place in a Christian drug rehabilitation program.

The only place they could find was in North Philadelphia near a holistic health center called Esperanza started by a very dear friend of mine, Dr. Carolyn Klaus. Esperanza's doctors and nurses offer both excellent health care and the love of Christ. Working closely with local Hispanic churches, they integrate evangelism and medicine.

Esperanza's Dr. Mike Moore became Juan's doctor. When Dr. Moore first met Juan in January 1992, Juan was ill and depressed. That busy day, Dr. Moore had just enough time to give Juan some medicine and say a couple words of encouragement. He also gave Juan Scriptures selected for people with AIDS. At Juan's next visit a week later, Dr. Moore was surprised to find Juan visibly changed. Moore discovered that John 3:16 had spoken powerfully to Juan's heart.

Dr. Moore walked closely with Juan over the next few months. He offered medicine, counsel, and prayer. Dr. Moore prayed that God would do what he could not. Soon Juan stopped praying for healing. Instead, he was content to ask God just to be "preserved."

The earlier doctor's warning that Juan would not live to see another birthday proved wrong. God gave him three more years–and Juan used them to minister in a powerful, loving way to others dying of AIDS.

Juan learned how to read so he could study the Bible. Then he hit the streets. But he was a changed person. On the street corners and in the parks, he told others about how Jesus had transformed his life. He visited people dying of AIDS in the hospital to bring encouragement and invite people to Christ. Dr. Moore sometimes asked Juan to visit other patients of his who were hospitalized with AIDS. Even when Juan himself had to be hospitalized, he continued to encourage other patients.

Finally, in the last few months of 1994, Juan himself became much sicker. But even during the final stay in the hospital, Juan continued to grow in his trust in God. When Dr. Moore asked Juan what was most important to remember about him, Juan said: "That God is real and that he is living in me." Juan died of AIDS on February 4, 1995. But as Dr. Moore says so powerfully, the Divine Healer had the last word: "When Juan's strength was gone and medicine had done all it could do, the Lord saw fit no longer to 'preserve' him here, but to heal him in his own presence."

It would have been so much better if Christians who love the whole person had gotten to Juan many years earlier. Then perhaps he would have had a long, full life of joy and wholeness like Cassandra and Showen Franklin. But even after HIV had begun its deadly march through Juan's body, the Divine Healer still worked powerfully—first to preserve Juan for three astonishing years of gentle, effective ministry here and then to heal him completely for joy unspeakable in the presence of the risen Lord.

7

MUST WE KNOCK DOWN OTHER PEOPLE'S CANDLES?

Characteristic Seven

Genuine Christians mourn church divisions and embrace all who confess Jesus as God and Savior

I watched a sad spectacle as I stood by Jesus' empty tomb on Easter morning 1993. My wife, Arbutus, and I had wandered into the massive Church of the Holy Sepulcher in Jerusalem, probably erected in the place where Jesus was prepared for burial and placed in the tomb. As wide-eyed pilgrims unfamiliar with the schedules (and ecclesiastical conflicts) of the ancient church, we joined a large crowd of people in front of the stone memorial built over the original tomb and watched as a Roman Catholic cardinal led an Easter service.

Part way through the celebration, Israeli police suddenly began clearing a path at the edge of the crowd. Behind them marched a group of Orthodox Christians loudly celebrating Jesus' triumphal entry into Jerusalem.

The Catholics celebrating Easter had lit dozens of small candles around the outside of the empty tomb. Suddenly an Orthodox priest stalked over to these candles and knocked them all down, snuffing out their flickering flames with quick, angry strokes.

Amazed, I walked over and hesitantly asked him why.

"Because candles are forbidden," he retorted.

"By whom?" I wondered.

"By me," came his annoyed reply.

I tried to explain that I wasn't being critical; I merely wanted to understand. So I persisted: "Is it always forbidden to light candles here, or just sometimes?"

"Not until next Sunday," he explained. This was still Palm Sunday in the Orthodox Church calendar. Candles could be lit again only at Easter. If the Catholics considered Palm Sunday to be Easter, so much the worse for them, their calendar, and their candles.

Reminders of the brokenness of Christ's body are everywhere in the Holy Land. For many decades, a Muslim family has kept the key to the Church of the Holy Sepulcher because Christians cannot agree among themselves on who should "control" this hallowed ground.

I do not mean to place all the blame on Catholics and Orthodox. Evangelical Protestants come to the land of Jesus' birth and almost totally ignore the present Christian (largely Palestinian) local church.

I was overcome with sadness as the meaning of this little tragedy swept over me. Arbutus and I quietly walked to the large slab of marble where, according to tradition, the mourners laid Jesus to prepare his body for burial. I joined the people kneeling there and began to sob. Others kneeling there were also weeping—in sympathy, I suppose, as they remembered the way Roman crucifixion had torn and broken Jesus' body on the cross. I wept over the ghastly tragedy of contemporary Christians desecrating his one body today with our petty disputes and stubbornly held traditions.

I felt the scandal of our brokenness in a new painful way that morning. I experienced our division as terrible disobedience and ghastly sin for which we must repent. Kneeling near the empty tomb that Easter, I knew my risen Lord was calling me to a deeper commitment to seek healing of the divisions in his one body.

I do not mean we should ignore major theological differences. We must remain faithful to biblical truth. Never dare we do what A. W. Tozer warned vividly against: "Truth is slain to provide a feast to celebrate the marriage of heaven and hell."[1]

But Christians are called to unity and love as well as to truth. Pointedly, persistently, the New Testament urges us to do everything in our power to avoid disunity. Why? There is just one body of Christ because there is only one gospel (Gal. 1:6–9), one salvation (Acts 4:12), one revelation (1 Cor. 2:6–10), one Lord's Supper (1 Cor. 10:17), and one Lord. "Make every effort to keep the unity of the Spirit through the bond of peace. There is one body and one Spirit—just as you were called to one hope when you were called—one Lord, one faith, one baptism; one God and Father of all" (Eph. 4:3–6). There are many different gifts in the body, but their common purpose is to build up that one body "until we all reach unity in the faith" (v. 13).

Jesus established one church, not a shopping mall of denominations. The New Testament uses the singular word *church* to refer to all who believe in Jesus Christ (1 Cor. 10:32; Gal. 1:13).[2] Sometimes the kinds of attitudes and actions that later produced denominational divisions reared their ugly head in the early church. Just as regularly, the New Testament denounced them harshly.[3] Factionalism, (1 Cor. 1:10–17), lust for power (Phil. 2:1–11), and refusal to seek reconciliation (Matt. 18:15–20) are all sin. When Paul learned of the warring factions in Corinth, he begged the Christians there to "agree with one another so that there may be no divisions among you and that you may be perfectly united in mind and thought" (1 Cor. 1:10). "Is Christ divided?" Paul asks in horror. The very existence of denominations is a mark of our failure and sin.

Nowhere is the call to love and unity in the body of Christ put more powerfully than in Jesus' final prayer for the church. Jesus specifically prays for Christians through the ages, pleading with God to give them such complete unity that the world may believe.

> My prayer is not for them alone. I pray also for those who will believe in me through their message, that all of them may be one, Father, just as you are in me and I am in you. May they also be in us so that the world may believe that you have sent me. I have given them the glory that you gave me, that they may be one as we are one: I in them and you in me. May they be brought to complete unity to let the world know that you sent me and have loved them even as you have loved me.
>
> John 17:20–23

How can we listen to this final prayer of our Lord and not weep? Christ's one body has been ripped apart into thousands of pieces. We have divided over things as petty as clothing fashions and musical preferences. Precisely the racial and economic divisions that Paul said the gospel was meant to overcome now divide us (1 Cor. 11:17–33; Eph. 2–3). If we care at all about our Lord's final prayer, we will resolve anew to work for Christian unity.

Jesus' prayer prevents us from reaching for some cheap, easy solution to our brokenness. It would be simple if we could just say that all genuine Christians enjoy invisible spiritual unity. To a certain extent, of course, that is true.

But the very words of Jesus' prayer prevent us from resting satisfied with some vague invisible unity. Jesus specifically prays that our unity will convince the world that he came from the Father. The world cannot see *invisible* unity! Only when we clearly, concretely, publicly demonstrate that all Christians are one can the world see and believe.

There is only one faithful conclusion for serious Christians. Unless we want to defy Jesus' final prayer for us, we must resolve to make Christian unity an urgent priority.

Repentance is the place to start. From all the shattered fragments of Christ's divided body, we must cry out together: "Our divisions are a scandal, an abomination, a damnable sin against you, O Lord. Have mercy upon us."

It is a sin to refuse to participate in ecumenical dialogue and fellowship with all other Christians who confess Jesus Christ as God and Savior according to the Scriptures. It is a sin to send missionaries to other lands without first consulting carefully with the Christians already there. It is a sin not to work hard and pray fervently to overcome the denominational divisions, theological disagreements, and ethical arguments that divide Christians.

After repentance for our brokenness and a firm resolve to seek unity, perhaps the best thing we can do is ponder long over how much all major branches of Christianity have in common. Protestant, Orthodox, and Roman Catholic Christians do disagree on some significant points. But on the central points, the historic confessions of all these Christian traditions agree! We all confess that there is one God–Father, Son, and Holy Spirit. We all believe that Jesus Christ is true God and true man. We all teach that sin separates us from God and that Jesus Christ is the only way to salvation for all people everywhere. We all confess that the Bible is God's divinely inspired, authoritative revelation, not a mere human book. We all look forward to that coming day when the returning Christ will complete the victory over sin and death and the kingdoms of this world will become the kingdom of our Lord.

In addition to those central doctrines, we also share basic components of the biblical worldview. Some non-Christian Eastern religions see the world around us as an illusion that we should escape. Modern secularists view it as the accidental result of cosmic chance. Christians, however, agree that creation is a good gift from a loving Creator. Modern materialists see humans as no more important than monkeys or moles. Christians agree that humans alone bear the divine image. Therefore, every human being is immeasurably valuable. Modern secularists suppose that human life is just a passing flicker of consciousness after which we pass into sheer nothingness. Christians agree that life here, however good, is just the beginning of life eternal in the presence of the living God. However much we may still debate the details, there are fundamental biblical perspectives on persons and society that Catholic, Orthodox, and Protestant Christians share.

Of course, we must continue to discuss our genuine disagreements over things like the Eucharist, infant baptism, the role of Mary and the saints, the status of church tradition, and the authority of the bishop of Rome. But is it not exceedingly important that at every moment of that ongoing debate, we keep clearly in mind that we stand together in our belief in the Trinity, the deity of Jesus Christ, and salvation through Christ alone?

But what about those who claim to be Christian and reject even the most basic Christian confession that Jesus is true God as well as true man? What about all the nominal Christians whose faith seems to be more ethnic identity or cultural baggage than genuine faith? All these questions and many more demand answers.

My plea for Christian unity is grounded in the central confession that Jesus the carpenter is true God. In his Gospel, John abhors church divisions (1 John 2:18–19), but he also denounces as antichrist and rejects Christian fellowship with anyone who denies that Jesus Christ has come in the flesh (4:13). Confession of the full deity and humanity of Christ is the indispensable foundation for Christian unity.

Furthermore, we certainly should invite lukewarm and nominal Christians, no matter what their church tradition, to experience the joy of a personal living relationship with Christ. But half-hearted, nominal Christians don't exist only in Roman Catholic and Eastern Orthodox circles. They are also Baptists, Mennonites, Presbyterians, Anglicans, and Methodists. Nor should we urge people to join our particular congregation or denomination just because God has given us the glorious privilege of helping them move to a vital, living faith. God may want them to work for renewal within their own tradition.

What should we do after we have repented and reminded ourselves that we agree on the most basic things? An important next step is to sort through the places where we do differ and distinguish between differences that we believe are very important and differences that are not.[4]

Many differences are relatively insignificant. Thus far in my walk with Christ, lighting candles at places like the empty tomb has not been a means of spiritual devotion and growth. But please God, let me listen long, with loving care and patience, before I knock down other group's candles. We can be truly one in Christ and gladly affirm the right of other Christians to use liturgical practices, musical styles, and artistic forms that differ from ours.

Sometimes for the sake of Christian unity, we should change what we do even when it is valid in itself. What a tragedy that Christians around the world fight with each other over what they believe is the correct day to celebrate our Savior's resurrection. I would gladly celebrate Easter according to the calendar of the Eastern Orthodox for the next hundred years if all Christians around the world could do it together.

What about the substantial disagreements? We dare not pretend they do not exist. I deeply respect the Roman Catholic bishop of Rome. In fact, I often agree with the official statements by Pope John Paul II. But I cannot accept papal infallibility. In spite of the best efforts of careful theologians, we still disagree over the role of the Virgin Mary, transubstantiation, and purgatory. What do we do? These differences are too great to ignore. They are even too big to permit organizational union.

It is at this point that we must sadly, temporarily, accept different denominations even as we confess that denominations are not God's will. We are all finite and limited—and also still sinful. Therefore, we only partially grasp the full truth of God's revelation in the Bible. As I look back in church history, I discover that even the best Christian theologians like Augustine and Luther sometimes made theological mistakes. Surely therefore, you and I—and all our contemporaries—are failing at least as often in our struggle to submit to God's Word. That should make us humble. It also makes me cling a little less tightly to my present theological understanding. But I cannot abandon what I believe is clear biblical teaching just because other Christians disagree.

By all means we should listen long and hard to all Christians—both those from previous centuries and contemporaries in all places. As I do that, I discover that the central affirmations of historic Christianity over the centuries flow from and agree with God's revelation. But always the Bible—prayerfully interpreted with the guidance of the Holy Spirit in dialogue with all Christians—is the norm.

Tragically we are still too stubborn and sinful to reach the theological unity that the God of the Scriptures desires. Therefore, we must live in the temporary, makeshift shelters we call denominations. We should always be dissatisfied with them. But until we can reach greater agreement, we must affirm their temporary, partial legitimacy.

That means that local congregations and clusters of congregations joined together in denominations should agree on what they believe the Bible calls them to teach and do. Presbyterians (at least historically) have thought that included predestination. Wesleyans disagree. Mennonites believe Jesus taught us never to kill. "Just War" Christians honestly conclude that there are exceptions. Local congregations and denominations rightly formulate what is their most faithful understanding of God's Word as they pray, seek the Spirit, and dialogue with the full body of Christ. Therefore, they should insist that membership in that congregation or denomination means acceptance of those specific items of belief and practice that they believe the Scriptures clearly teach to be important.

But that does not mean that Calvinists who think the Wesleyan understanding of free will is wrong or that Mennonites who believe that Just War Christians have seriously misunderstood Jesus should have nothing to do with each other. To conclude that would be to forget that we all believe in the same triune God, all confess the deity and humanity of Christ, and all trust in salvation through Christ alone.

To overlook or belittle this underlying unity is scandalous sin that breaks God's heart. Christians today are in rebellious disobedience to the Lord we worship if we are not ready to publicly, visibly demonstrate our unity with all Christians who confess the basic truths of historic Christianity.

What is the minimal confession that we must share? We could use the Apostles' Creed from the early church. Or we could take the WCC's official confession: "The World Council of Churches is a fellowship of churches which confess the Lord Jesus Christ as God and Savior according to the Scriptures and therefore seek to fulfill together their common calling to the glory of the one God, Father, Son and Holy Spirit."[5]

Is that not enough? How can anyone accept Jesus' prayer in John 17:23 and refuse to fellowship with those who confess the Lord Jesus Christ as God and Savior according to the Scriptures? I want to argue with many things the WCC does. I also want to challenge many things many Roman Catholics, Eastern Orthodox, Pentecostals, mainline Protestants, and evangelicals say and do! But if they truly confess my Lord Jesus as God and Savior according to the Scriptures, they are my beloved sisters and brothers in Christ.

That means that I am called to join them in visibly implementing Jesus' prayer in John 17. I am called to demonstrate the kind of loving unity with them that will convince surrounding society that Jesus came from the Father. And unless today's skeptics are much easier to convince than in the past, that means that Jesus summons every Christian, every congregation, and every denomination to take new concrete steps to demonstrate the biblical truth that Christ's body is one.

There are at least five different levels on which we could express Christian unity in new ways:

1. *Closer personal friendship with other Christians.* We all regularly meet Christians from other traditions at school, work, sports, and around our homes. What would happen if our first thought in each such situation was always: "Here is a sister or brother who believes in the same God, worships the same Lord Jesus, and trusts the same Redeemer for their salvation. This common bond is more important than all the things that divided us. So how can I make our unity so visible that it will draw unbelievers to the Lord we both adore?" If we did that, we would probably talk more openly about our faith with Christian neighbors and Christian colleagues at work. We would probably share joys and sorrows more often. We would probably help each other deal with problems and visit each others' homes and churches more frequently. Unbelieving neighbors might notice and like what they see.

2. *Cooperative coalitions with other Christians to shape public life.* Such Christian cooperation is urgently needed.

In the United States, 86 percent of the adult population claims to be Christian. But you would never guess that to be true if you only looked at the way secular ideas have flourished in politics, the arts, the media, and the law over the last thirty years. Part of the problem, of course, is that Christians themselves disagree on many tough issues of public life. Partly, however, our ineffectiveness results from the fact that the different Christian groups have not yet learned how to work together even when they agree on the basic direction public policy should take.

In recent years, there have been some important breakthroughs. Evangelical Protestants and Roman Catholics have worked together to oppose abortion on demand. More recently, evangelicals, mainline Protestants, and Catholics have cooperated in the National Religious Partnership on the Environment.[6] In 1994, a number of evangelical and Catholic leaders including Charles Colson, Bill Bright, Cardinal O'Connor, James I. Packer, Richard J. Neuhaus, and Ralph Martin issued a joint call, "Evangelicals and Catholics Together," urging Evangelicals and Catholics to work together to shape public policy.[7]

The faith that Protestant, Catholic, and Orthodox believers all share tells us that our society will be better if we renew marriage and family life, empower the poor, respect the sanctity of human life, care for creation, oppose pornography, work for peaceful alternatives to violence, and reduce sex and violence in the media. Surely our children would benefit and the Lord of history would be honored if all Christian groups found better ways to cooperate to make our common life more wholesome, decent, and just.

3. *Cooperative, informal activities for specifically Christian endeavors.* Billy Graham has pioneered broad Christian cooperation in the area of evangelism. For decades, he has invited Catholics, Orthodox believers, and a wide variety of Protestants to participate in his city-wide evangelistic crusades. Dr. Graham never compromises his message.

But he gladly welcomes a wide diversity of Christians to join together in his large crusades. Billy Graham's crusades have probably done as much as any other single factor to create mutual understanding and growing trust among Christians.

Graham's approach works because it is informal. The Billy Graham Association is not a local congregation or denomination. Therefore individual Christians from many different traditions can join together to share Christ with their city.

Could we not expand what Billy Graham has started? Whether the concern is Christian schools, Christian media, Christian relief and development, or Christian evangelism, we should always ask: Could a broader range of Christians do this together better? Would our witness to non-Christians be more powerful if we cooperated on this with Christians from other traditions? Would the additional struggles be worth the benefits? Would the broader participation sharpen our witness and heighten our impact? Or would it water down the message and undermine the results? Those questions are not easy to answer. But we should always have Jesus' prayer for unity ringing in our ears as we struggle for answers.

4. *Formal fellowships or councils of congregations and denominations.* Informal cooperation is important, but it is no substitute for formal interaction in fellowships, alliances, and councils of churches.

Evangelical Protestants were the early leaders in ecumenical cooperation. The Evangelical Alliance in England, formed in 1846, brought together evangelical Christians from many Protestant denominations. In this century, parallel groups like the National Association of Evangelicals in the United States and the Evangelical Fellowship of Canada have sprung up in dozens of countries. Today, more than 110 regional and national evangelical fellowships or alliances in over 105 countries belong to the World Evangelical Fellowship. Individuals, congregations, and denominations that share the national evangelical fellowship's statement on theology and mission work together to increase understanding, witness to Christ, and serve the world.

Somewhat different in structure and approach are the national councils of churches and the World Council of Churches. Composed of member denominations, these councils seek to promote Christian unity and do together what is better done cooperatively. Evangelical Protestants, including myself, have often been critical of specific programs and statements of the WCC. Too often evangelism has been neglected and solid theological foundations have been ignored. Many evangelical denominations, as a result, have refused to join the WCC.

Should evangelical Christians continue that stance? I cannot see how we can and continue to submit to what the New Testament teaches about the unity of Christ's body. How can we fail to fellowship with other Christians who confess Jesus Christ as God and Savior according to the Scriptures? Of course there are important areas of disagreement. It may be true that some who participate in the programs of the WCC do not truly believe the WCC's doctrinal foundation. But think of how different the programs and statements of the WCC would have been over the past few decades if all evangelicals worldwide had been active participants.

Perhaps the ideal next step would be for Protestant, Orthodox, and Catholic Christians to begin a process together to form new kinds of ecumenical councils in each nation and the world. That seems like an impossible task. But if we worship the same God and trust for our salvation in the same Savior, how dare we refuse to join together to form councils for the purpose of talking honestly about our differences, seeking truly for greater unity, and cooperating where possible in what God has called us to do? To refuse to do all we can to answer our Lord's prayer is disobedience and sin.

5. *Organizational union.* This, finally, is the toughest task. Not all denominational mergers are right. Biblical theology must always be the foundation. More effective evangelism and service must be the result. The process must be careful and open lest one merger spark a new division.

But is there really any adequate reason for different Baptist or Presbyterian or Mennonite denominations with very similar theology to remain separate rather than unite? John Frame rightly deplores the situation where two Presbyterian churches remain apart even though they agree on almost everything except that the one uses only the Psalms for singing in worship.[8] How long dare we let different histories, diverse cultural patterns, false fears, and leadership positions keep us from organizational union among groups whose theology is overwhelmingly similar? Surely, in such cases, the burden of proof rests with those who want to remain separate.

Sadly I must confess that apart from dramatic divine intervention, I do not expect great progress in the near future. Even the modest proposals of the recent "Evangelicals and Catholics Together" met with harsh denunciation. Embracing both truth and unity will never be easy for finite, imperfect pilgrims.

No matter what the cost, however, faithful disciples seek to be obedient to Jesus. It is God become flesh who calls us to unity. It is our Savior who prays that we forsake our sinful divisions. It is our risen Lord who promises that Christians can now by his mighty power display such astonishing love and unity that the world may believe.

O Lord, help Christians today to resolve anew to open themselves without reservation to be a part of the answer to your final prayer for the church.

Part 3

THE WORLD

8

Bedroom, Boardroom, and Ballot Box

Characteristic Eight

Genuine Christians confess that Jesus is Lord of politics
and economics

Is Jesus Lord of the boardroom as well as the bedroom? Is
Jesus Lord of the Congress just as much as the church? Does
Jesus care as much about how you vote as how you pray?
As much about how you work as how you worship? As much
about public as private life?

William Wilberforce thought so. As a young, wealthy aris-
tocrat in eighteenth-century England, Wilberforce lived the
worldly, indulgent life of an up-and-coming member of
Parliament. But he was powerfully converted in the Wes-

leyan revival. Turning from the social whirl of frivolity and excess, Wilberforce dedicated his gifts and position as a politician to God's cause. He never thought that becoming a dedicated Christian required him to give up his political career, for he was convinced that "with a perfect regard to my duty to God, myself and my fellows, I was bound to do it."[1] For over forty years he was the leading crusader against slavery in the British House of Commons.

Politics was not Wilberforce's only passion. He was also engaged in evangelism. One of his most important books was a plea to the British upper classes to become committed Christians, and he and his friends actively promoted foreign missionary work around the world.

Wilberforce's primary calling, however, was politics. He believed that God had brought him to political power to end the ghastly evil of the slave trade and slavery. Over the years, untold millions of "pagan" Africans died from rape, starvation, torture, and sharks on the way to the brave new world of "Christians." The "lucky" five to ten million who survived the journey had to endure being whipped and bred like animals.[2]

In 1787, when Wilberforce began his crusade, slave ships from "Christian" Europe carried one hundred thousand captured Africans to the Americas every year. In fact, Wilberforce's England was the leader in this savage tyranny, with British ships carrying one-half of this human cargo.[3] The huge profits represented a significant part of the British economy.

But Wilberforce knew slavery was a terrible sin against God and neighbor–even though almost all respectable people of his time quietly accepted the prevailing view that slaves were just property to be bought and sold like coal and cattle. Wilberforce prayed and lobbied. In fact, his small circle of friends regularly prayed three hours a day for their many tasks, including their crusade to abolish the slave trade and slavery.

Wilberforce was a brilliant political organizer. He had to be, because his opponents insisted that abolishing the slave trade would destroy the British economy. Wilberforce's response was to say that people and ethics matter more than money and profit. After a twenty-year struggle, the British Parliament finally abolished the slave trade in 1807. Twenty-six years later, in the very year Wilberforce died, the British Parliament abolished slavery itself. Slowly, over the next century, the rest of the world did the same.

Wilberforce was the central player in this momentous change in world history. He did it all because of Christ—because he knew Jesus was Lord of politics and economics. So many modern Christians do not understand that. For many, Jesus has little to do with how they vote or run their business. They have developed a privatized, individualistic understanding of religion. Faith only relates to personal life in the family and to church on Sunday. Church and maybe sexual practices belong to the spiritual realm. Politics and economics belong to the secular.

How could this have happened to Christians who claim that Jesus is Lord of all? It happened slowly in Western culture. In the Middle Ages, everybody understood that theology was the queen of all learning and that every area of life should submit to Christ and divine revelation. They did not always practice what they preached, but in theory Christian faith was to shape every part of society.

Everything slowly changed with the astounding success of modern science. Scientists made amazing progress in discovering how nature regularly works. Scientists discovered natural, scientific explanations for many things medieval people had explained as miracles. Scientists, for example, realized that plagues and comets did not happen because God was angry, as people in the Middle Ages thought. These natural events had natural causes. Then in the eighteenth century, some thinkers jumped from the fact that most things have a scientific explanation to the very different claim that everything has a scientific explanation. In fact, they argued, nothing is real or true except what science can measure or describe. Obviously, we can not measure God in the laboratory or the spaceship. This new radical secular view rejected God and miracles and placed human beings with their new science and technology at the center of the world.

At first Christians rejected this secular humanism. But they failed to see how the effect of science and technology was slowly undermining the Christian claim that Christ is Lord of all and quietly reducing Christian faith to a little private world of personal belief. They missed the subtle ways that the secular perspective was sneaking into pious hearts and orthodox minds.

Science and technology proved to be incredibly powerful. First water power, then fossil fuels, and then nuclear reactors replaced the muscles of horses and people. The result was an explosion of production. More and more products at vastly lower prices per hour of human effort flowed from farms and factories. The telegraph, radio, television, and E-mail revolutionized communication. Evermore powerful microchips and sophisticated computers have revolutionized everything. At the core still stands a triumphant science and technology.

God seems unnecessary in scientific labs, in factories run by robots and computers, in advertising firms. Economics has became a science and explains how the economy works. And work it does in Western free markets. In just forty years from 1950 to 1990, the world produced more goods than in all of human history up to that point. Rational scientific thought is all you need, many people feel, to run the economy, the government, and the ongoing scientific revolution.

Religious faith is still okay, as long as you keep it private– at church once or twice a week and at home. But it certainly has no business interfering with politics and economics–

public arenas based on rational, scientific thought, not private belief.

Incredibly, many Christians accept–even gladly embrace–this radical emasculation and privatization of historic Christianity.[4] Many Christians enjoy vast new wealth produced by this astonishingly creative combination of technology and capitalism, and indeed there are many wonderful benefits, including improved education, health care, and more than enough food, clothing, and housing for all. Many Christians quietly accept the way things are without asking whether everybody benefits fairly from the new abundance in a way that would please God–who cares especially for the poorest.

In fact, some Christians have even developed a theology to justify this privatization of religious faith. Incredibly, evangelical Christians especially endorse this privatized faith produced by the new secularism and modernization. For many evangelicals, faith deals with spiritual things like evangelism, personal devotions, worship, and family. The only way to change the world, they believe, is through individual conversion. It is only the worldly, liberal Christians, many evangelicals argue, who mess with politics and worry about whether the economic system might displease God. Only "secular" Christians try to improve the world by changing social structures.

The Bible sees things in a radically different way. The first Christians were just a minuscule handful of believers in a vast pagan empire. But they dared to announce to the whole world that the crucified and risen carpenter they worshiped and followed was now "ruler of the kings of the earth" (Rev. 1:5). When Jesus' demands clashed with those of Caesar, they followed Jesus because they knew he was "far above all rule and authority, power and dominion" (Eph. 1:21). They could never forget that Jesus reminded Pilate that his power came from God (John 19:11). They believed Jesus' final words, "All authority in heaven and on earth has been given to me" (Matt. 28:18). Knowing that, they sought to govern every area of their lives by the standards of Jesus' dawning kingdom.

That belief had concrete practical implications for how they spent their money. Jesus had warned pointedly that they could not worship God and wealth (Matt. 6:24). Paul insisted that greed was really idolatry. Imagine how it would transform the lives of Christians today if we truly believed Paul's warning that economic greed is just as terrible as sexual sin. "Among you there must not be even a hint of sexual immorality, or of any kind of impurity, or of greed. . . . No immoral, impure or greedy person–such a man is an idolater–has any inheritance in the kingdom of Christ" (Eph. 5:3–5). The early Christians actually lived that way. "No one claimed that any of his possessions was his own, but they shared everything they had" (Acts 4:32). That does not mean they abolished private property. But it does mean they understood the implications of their central confession. Christ is Lord, and that includes money and economics.

Nor was the conviction that every sphere and every realm belongs to God some new revelation. Everywhere in the Old Testament we meet the sweeping declaration that there is one God who rules all the nations and all spheres of life. Even when they do not recognize it, foreign conquerors and marching armies move at God's command (Isa. 44:28). Economics, just as surely as politics, submits to the command of Yahweh. God owns the cattle on a thousand hills (Ps. 50:10). God could divide the land fairly among the families of Israel and then command them to return the land to the original owners every fifty years because the "land is mine and you are but aliens and my tenants" (Lev. 25:23). The biblical teaching is crystal clear. God is Lord of all, and that includes politics and economics.

One reason Christians have adopted a watered-down, privatized substitute for genuine faith is that they neglect the full biblical teaching about sin. Contrary to the Scriptures, some modern Christians see sin almost exclusively in personal terms. Sin means things like lying, stealing, drunkenness, and adultery. Now those things are wrong, terribly wrong. But so are racism and economic oppression.

The biblical understanding of sin emphasizes both personal and social sin. Amos announced God's wrath both against those who trample the poor and those who commit sexual misconduct (2:6-7). Isaiah shouted God's woe against those who deprive the poor of their land and homes and also those who fall into drunkenness (5:8-11, 22-23). In Amos 5, God explicitly condemned those who participate in an unjust legal system:

> You hate the one who reproves in court
> and despise him who tells the truth.
> You trample on the poor
> and force him to give you grain.
> Therefore, though you have built stone mansions,
> you will not live in them. . . .
> For I know how many are your offenses
> and how great your sins.
> You oppress the righteous and take bribes
> and you deprive the poor of justice in the courts.

vv. 10-12

According to the Bible, laws themselves are sometimes unjust because wicked leaders write and manipulate them for their selfish advantage. The psalmist denounced those who ally themselves with wicked rulers who legislate "mischief by statute" (Ps. 94:20 RSV). God speaks bluntly about unfair systems: "Woe to those who make unjust laws, to those who issue oppressive decrees, to deprive the poor of their rights and withhold justice from the oppressed of my people" (Isa. 10:1-2). In fact, God is so angry with people who profit from unjust systems that he sometimes destroys them. Amos said the wealthy women of his day would be dragged out of the city with huge hooks in their noses. Why? "Hear this word, you cows . . . , you women who oppress the poor and crush the needy and say to your husbands, 'Bring us some drinks!'" (Amos 4:1–2).

According to the Bible, participating in unfair legal systems and unjust economic structures is wrong and displeasing to God. Robbing your employees of a fair wage is just as evil as robbing a bank.

An Indian bishop once told me a story that underlines the importance of understanding social sin. There used to be a mental institution in India, he said, which had a fascinating way of deciding whether inmates were well enough to go home. They would take a person over to a water tap, place a large water bucket under the tap, and fill the bucket with water. Then, leaving the tap on, they would give the person a spoon and say, "Please empty the bucket." If the person started dipping the water out one spoonful at a time and never turned the tap off, they knew he was still crazy!

Too often Christians work at social problems one spoonful at a time. Too often we fail to ask how we can turn the tap off by changing legal systems and economic policies that hurt people. Of course we must lead individuals to Christ one person at a time. But understanding social sin helps us see more clearly how we can also improve society by reforming unfair systems and structures like slavery. It also enables us to grasp more fully the implications of Christ's lordship over politics and economics.

"Christ is Lord" is the most basic Christian confession. If Christians today want to be biblical, then we must rediscover what that means for our politics and economics. How do we do that?

Without any doubt, the single most important thing we must do is to surrender our thinking totally and unconditionally to biblical truth. We must cast our inherited political ideas, nationalistic biases, and treasured ideologies of left and right at the foot of the cross. The last thing our world needs is Christians in politics who claim to follow Jesus but really are captive to some left-wing or right-wing secular ideology.

Is it not strange when liberal Christian activists who deplore the starvation of many innocent children turn around and defend the annual destruction of millions of unborn babies? Is it not equally puzzling when prominent pro-life leaders promote the sale of tobacco, which kills just as surely as the abortionist's scalpel? Is the Bible setting their agenda? Or is it some secular political idea?

If Jesus is to be Lord of our politics, then he must write the platform. That means two things. First, it means adopting a biblically balanced agenda rather than a one-sided preoccupation with just one issue. The God revealed in Scripture cares about the poor and the family, about the sanctity of life and peace, about the unborn and the creation, about freedom and justice. Anybody who claims to be a Christian in politics should care about all the things God does.

Second, committed Christians should seek a genuinely biblical approach to *each* issue. That is easy to say. It is harder to do. God wants to empower the poor. But is that done better through a free market or a socialist system? I believe that a market economy corresponds better to biblical principles. But it simply will not do to blindly jump to that conclusion without carefully examining what the Bible says.

For more than a decade now, I have worked with an international network of evangelical leaders. We have gone back together to the Scriptures to seek out the crucial biblical principles relevant to economic life. I will never forget one long flight over the stormy North Atlantic on the way to one of our major conferences. As I sat there assigning people to the small groups, the vast range of contradictory viewpoints drove me to despair, and I had little hope of reaching any meaningful agreement. But we prayed and listened. Above all, we wanted to submit our hearts and minds to Christ and the Bible, and as a result, we formulated a statement on Christian faith and economics that I believe is biblical.[5]

Christians need to do the same for every issue in public life. If we are to promote a genuinely Christian policy on the family, the environment, or any other issue, we must carefully explore every relevant biblical text on the topic. After that, we need to summarize all the biblical material in an integrated framework or set of principles on that specific topic.[6]

Is that all we need to let Christ shape our politics? Unfortunately, no. I have never discovered a single word in the Bible about nuclear reactors, the ozone layer, or the World Bank. But we have to know about those complex modern realities in order to care for the environment and the poor in ways that are wise and biblical.

We have to study the modern world as well as the Bible. In order to apply biblical principles to our complex modern society, we have to examine history, economics, sociology, and politics. There is simply no substitute for careful, sophisticated socioeconomic analysis if we want to wisely implement biblical principles in society today. Too often Christians rush into politics without ever doing their homework. The result? We often look silly. Worse, we fail. Careful social analysis is essential.

That does not mean that we dare not vote unless we have completed five years of study in economics and politics! It does mean that we need the help of other Christians who are thinking responsibly about political issues. We need the assistance of organizations like Evangelicals for Social Action, which does careful study on specific political problems to help Christians today integrate biblical principles and precise, accurate social analysis.[7]

So far, I have talked about two crucial things that go into every political judgment: ethical principles and social analysis. As a Christian, I want to get my ethical principles from God's revelation. As for social analysis, I learn from anyone who thinks carefully and gets the "facts" straight.

But are biblical principles and accurate analysis all we need? Not quite. A political philosophy is also essential. Earlier I warned against jumping into politics with unexamined ideological prejudices. But that does not mean we do not need a political philosophy (that is what some people mean by ideology). Why? Because it is simply impossible to go back and do all the necessary work on biblical principles and social analysis every time we cast a ballot, evaluate a political speech, or lobby our senator. If we did that, it would take us decades to prepare for each election!

We need a short summary, a basic framework of principles and conclusions that helps us make specific, speedy political judgments. That framework is what I call a political philosophy or ideology. If we simply accept the political philosophy of our parents and friends, we may unconsciously adopt left-wing or right-wing or New Age ideas that contradict biblical faith. So an *unexamined* political philosophy is dangerous. An *examined* political philosophy, on the other hand, is a must.

How do we acquire a carefully constructed political philosophy? A valid, examined political philosophy develops when we combine biblical principles with careful analysis of history, economics, and politics.

Let me offer an illustration by briefly sketching my political philosophy. You don't have to agree. In fact, I urge you to be critical. Nobody's political philosophy is divinely revealed or without errors. But I have tried very hard to develop it out of biblical study and close examination of the world. So if you disagree, please don't call me names. Just show me lovingly and precisely where I have misunderstood the Bible or the world.

Seven Short Principles
for a Political Philosophy

1. Everybody should have power, not just a few.

The decentralization of power is my first principle. There is both a negative and a positive reason for democratization or decentralization of power. Centralized power is dangerous because sinful people will almost always use concentrated power for themselves rather than everyone. In a fallen world, "Power corrupts and absolute power corrupts absolutely," as Lord Acton once said. Centralized power is also wrong because the Creator calls each person to be a coworker with almighty God as a steward of creation and a shaper of history. If only a handful of powerful people make all the decisions, most people cannot fulfill God's creation mandate.

As I examine history carefully, especially the twentieth century, I see totalitarian societies that have centralized power and democratic nations that have substantially decentralized it. It is painfully obvious that the ghastly evil of Marxist societies was directly related to the fact that they placed almost all power, both political and economic, in the hands of a few. The State owned everything and the elite of the Communist Party controlled the State.

Private ownership and democratic institutions are good systems to decentralize power. The more all persons share in the ownership of economic resources, the more economic power is distributed. A friend of mine likes to say that private property is so good that God wants everyone to have some! When everyone has the vote in a genuinely free democracy, there is little danger of tyranny. Balancing federal power with state and local power; balancing legislative, judicial, and administrative power; and balancing government power with many private institutions free of government–all these things decentralize power. Both biblical principles and the experience of the modern world call for the decentralization and democratization of power. Doing that leads to both democratic government and a market economy.

That does not mean that today's democratic societies and market economies are perfect.[8] Tragic injustice continues to exist even in the best. Vast concentrations of power are present in today's huge government bureaucracies and massive multinational corporations. One of the most dangerous concentrations of power today lies with huge multinational corporations, with annual incomes larger than the total GNP of many entire countries. Individual nations can no longer restrain them. There is little check on their power except their own self-defined self-interest. One mark of biblical consistency today will be the courage to decentralize power wherever it is dangerously concentrated–whether in totalitarian governments or excessively large multinational corporations.

2. The poor deserve special care.

My second principle calls for a special concern for the poor. Literally hundreds of verses in the Bible remind us of God's special concern to lift up the poor. That does not mean God is biased toward the poor. God cares equally about everyone. But almost all the rich and powerful throughout history have cared a lot more about themselves than for the poor. By contrast with our bias, God's lack of bias looks like a bias! Precisely because God cares equally about everyone, God works in history to lift up the most neglected.

Christians in politics will do the same–if biblical principles rather than secular ideology rule their hearts. How much time did Jesus and the prophets spend defending their own interests or those of the rich and powerful? Watch carefully who it is that Christians in politics support and defend. Are they first of all a voice for the poor or a voice for the comfortable? Are they primarily looking out for their self-interest or the interests of the weak? Are they best known as voices of conscience, reminding everyone that God judges societies by what they do to people on the bottom?

3. Every person should have the capital to earn a decent living.

My third principle flows from my attempt to develop a biblical understanding of equality or equity.[9] Equity does not mean that everyone has identical income or wealth. But it does mean that everyone has access to the necessities of life that enable them to be dignified, participating members of their society. For most people, that means the opportunity to earn a decent living. For a few who are sick or disabled, it means–if we understand the sanctity of every human life–that family, friends, and society supply their needs.

The Old Testament teaching on the use of land helps us understand this third principle of equity. In an agricultural society, land was the basic capital, the basic source of wealth. So God divided the land more or less equally among the tribes and families (Num. 26:52–56; Josh. 18:1–7). Then God commanded the Jubilee so that every fifty years, land returned to the original owner no matter why they lost it (Lev. 25:1–29). God wanted each family to have the basic capital to earn their own way with dignity and responsibility.

At one time, that meant enabling every farmer to own forty acres and a mule. In a different society, the principle of equity means that everyone has a genuine opportunity for a job that pays a living wage or the capital to start a small business. In our information society, this principle calls for equality of educational opportunity because knowledge is the basic capital today.

How we can spot the politicians who are acting on biblical principles? They are the politicians that call on the rich and powerful to spend whatever it takes to offer the poorest citizens equal opportunity to acquire the capital necessary to earn their own way and become dignified participating members of their community.

4. Maintain the balance between freedom and justice.

My fourth principle refuses to play freedom off against economic justice. Both are important. Neither dare be subordinate to the other. Marxists used to invite us to sacrifice freedom for alleged justice. Some defenders of unrestricted capitalism wanted to subordinate economic justice to freedom. Biblical people will do neither. Both freedom and justice are essential.

5. Always think globally.

The fifth principle summons Christians to a global perspective rather than a narrow nationalism. The self-centered jingoism of much modern patriotism is simply sin. Because everyone in the world is our sister and brother on the basis of creation, and because every single person is so precious that our Savior would gladly die for them, Christians must be citizens of the world before we are citizens of a particular country. That does not mean that all patriotic love of a particular history and geography is wrong. Nor does it mean that a global perspective demands a centralized world government. It does, however, require that Christians resist nationalistic public policies that benefit their nation at the expense of others.

6. Protect the separation of church and state.

My sixth principle emphasizes the importance of separation of church and state. That does not mean that we should try to separate ethical or religious values from the political process. It does not mean that religious leaders should "stay out of politics." But it does mean that the state should not interfere with the free, independent functioning of religious institutions. Nor should the church look to the state to enforce Christian theology or write prayers for the schools.

7. Understand the limits of politics.

My last principle insists on the limitations of politics and economics. Political and economic change is not the only way to transform the world. It is not even the most important! Biblical people will never fall into the modern political illusion of supposing that we can create a brave new world merely through restructuring society.

Personal conversion can change hearts and transform characters in a deeper way than politics ever can. Cultural values shaped by religion, literature, art, and education are far more significant than temporary legislative victories that the next election may overturn. Faithful parents, honest journalists, and dedicated educators all shape society as profoundly as politicians. Structural change is only one way to change the world.

Biblical people never let political action take the place of evangelism. On the other hand, they never forget that the Lord they worship is also the Sovereign of politics. They will remember that God has used devoted Christian politicians like William Wilberforce to change world history.

Charles Finney was the leading evangelist of mid-nineteenth-century America. Thousands upon thousands of people came to Christ in his revival campaigns. Finney was also a leading abolitionist, and regularly in his revivals, he preached against the social sin of slavery. Modern historians have discovered that in several states the core of the abolitionist movement grew out of groups of people converted in Finney's revivals.

Finney spent half of each year as professor of theology at a newly founded evangelical college, Oberlin College, but he agreed to come only if Oberlin accepted African-American students. Oberlin agreed and became the first college in the United States to welcome African-Americans as regular students. Oberlin also rediscovered the biblical teaching on the dignity of women, becoming the first college in the United States to offer college degrees to women. In fact, evangelical Christians from Oberlin were key leaders in the first period of the feminist movement. Oberlin evangelicals played a central role both in abolishing slavery in America and gaining the vote for women in 1920.[10]

Finney could not have accomplished what he did without the financial support of the devout Tappan brothers—two of the most wealthy businessmen in New York. Arthur Tappan founded the *Journal of Commerce* in 1827, and Lewis Tappan established the forerunner of today's Dun and Bradstreet to provide credit ratings for business. Arthur lived modestly and pledged a huge part of his income to launch Oberlin College.

The Tappan brothers also played a central role in the funding and organizing of the abolitionist movement. They were hated in the South. One Southern minister offered a reward of $100,000 to anyone who would bring Arthur Tappan and the abolitionist editor he supported to New Orleans. When a Southern boycott of Tappan businesses threatened to spread to all Northern companies that traded with the Tappans, the New York business community panicked. They begged the Tappans to abandon their crusade against slavery. Arthur's response was blunt: "I will be hung first."[11]

Finney and the Tappans knew that politics was no sub-stitute for evangelism. They also knew that serious Christians submit their politics and economics to the living God.

Our world desperately needs a new movement of Christians who bring an uncompromisingly biblical perspective to political and economic life. Contemporary cynicism about government is so deep and pervasive that democracy itself is at risk. Divisions between rich and poor threaten to tear our world apart. Biblically informed political and economic leaders could change that.

Genuinely Christian politicians would stand out from the crowd—precisely because they follow a different drummer. They would be a voice for the voiceless and a model of integrity. They would understand both the possibilities and limitations of politics. They would add a humility and civility to political debate because they know everybody sometimes gets things wrong. They would not demonize opponents. They would not lob ideological half-truths that confuse rather than clarify public debate. They would seek honest dialogue rather than deceitful victory. They would seek truth and justice for all rather than power and privilege for a few.

Christian business leaders would be creative servants rather than dominating masters. They would use special talents and unusual wealth to create dignified jobs and important products for others. They would make a profit without worshiping the maximization of profit. They would value employees and creation more than the accumulation of wealth. They would risk hiring the poor and marginalized.[12]

Is it wishful dreaming to hope for a new generation of Christian politicians and business people like Wilberforce, Finney, and the Tappans? I do not think so. I believe there are people God is preparing for positions of prominence and power who are ready to look into the face of Christ and say: "By your grace, I will do anything that you want me to do."

A few hundred Wilberforces and Tappans could produce sweeping change in our world. They would not create Utopia. But they could bring dramatic reform. An underclass without jobs or capital could find new dignity and hope. Government could serve everyone, not just the powerful. Our world could become less divided, less violent, less unjust. The God of the poor would rejoice.

The world has yet to see what God would do if even a few thousand Christians would make this simple covenant with God: *I promise to submit every political act and every economic decision to your lordship.*

9

MOVING FROM THE CHAIR TO THE FLOOR

Characteristic Nine

Genuine Christians share God's special concern for the poor

Colleen and Vinay Samuel know what it means to move from the chair to the floor. Both grew up in well-to-do Indian homes. Both enjoyed an excellent education. When they returned to India after Vinay's doctoral study at Cambridge, Vinay pastored the most prestigious church in India's fastest growing city, Bangalore.

Successful ministry in this wealthy, influential congregation, however, could not silence their pain over the plight of the poor. In 1975, Colleen began to spend two hours a day in a slum called Lingarajapuram near Bangalore where poverty gnaws away at 70 percent of the people. First they started a school for children too poor to afford an education. Then came job training programs, an orphanage, a health clinic, small business development, micro-loans to tiny entrepreneurs, and a growing church.

In 1983, Vinay and Colleen astounded both their wealthy congregation and the slum dwellers in Lingarajapuram. Their whole family moved to Lingarajapuram. Forty thousand of their new neighbors live in tiny, one-room huts made of mud and leaves. The doorways are so small that you have to crawl in. Few of these huts have chairs. So when Vinay and Colleen visit, they sit on the floor just like their poor neighbors.

The results have been spectacular. Their multipronged community center now serves fifty thousand very needy people. Because prayer, worship, and evangelism are central to their ministry, they have led hundreds of people to Christ and started several new churches.[1]

This fantastic ministry would never have happened if Vinay and Colleen had not understood God's special concern for the poor and neglected. Because they understood and obeyed, God has used them to bless fifty thousand desperate neighbors. The same agonizing poverty that plagues Vinay and Colleen's community afflicts about one person out of every five alive today.[2] That's more than a billion people! They do not have enough food. Education and health care are almost nonexistent for them. Their children's brains often suffer permanent damage from lack of protein. Each day at least fifty thousand die of starvation, malnutrition, and preventable diseases.

At the same time, one person in four in our world lives and dies without ever once hearing about Jesus. Every day, about fifty thousand people enter eternity without being told about God's incredible love in Christ. Those dying without the knowledge of Christ are largely the same people whose lives are ravaged by hunger, malnutrition, and starvation.

Do Christians care that one-fifth to one-quarter of their neighbors are both desperately poor and without any knowledge of our Lord? Would the way we spend our money suggest an answer to that question? Christians make up one-third (33 percent) of the world's people, but we receive two-thirds (66 percent) of the world's total income each year. We spend 97 percent of that on ourselves. We donate about 2.5 percent to charity. And all but a tiny fraction of that charitable giving stays with rich Christians running expensive programs in their own congregations and nations.[3]

The gap between rich and poor is stark—and growing. In 1960, the income of the richest 20 percent of countries in the world was thirty times as much as the poorest 20 percent. By 1990, the richest 20 percent took sixty times as much as the poorest 20 percent.[4] Does it matter to God that even with growing wealth we give less than 3 percent to charity and spend most of that on ourselves?

The Bible says some explosive things about this question. Jesus' parable of the sheep and goats drives me to sober reflection every time I ponder it. To those who did not feed the hungry and clothe the naked, he will utter a terrible judgment: "Depart from me, you who are cursed, into the eternal fire prepared for the devil and his angels" (Matt. 25:41). The apostle John issues the same stark warning: "If anyone has material possessions and sees his brother in need but has no pity on him, how can the love of God be in him?" (1 John 3:17).[5]

The Bible is full of passages that underline God's special concern for the poor. There are literally hundreds of texts. I have collected them all in a book called *For They Shall Be Fed*.[6] Just the biblical passages on how God and God's faithful people love the poor filled up almost two hundred pages.

Four biblical truths about the poor are essential if the church today is to be faithful.

1. *Repeatedly, the Bible says that the Sovereign of history works to lift up the poor and oppressed.* That teaching is especially clear when we look at the central points of revelation history. Consider the Exodus. Certainly God acted there to keep the promise to Abraham and to call out the chosen people of Israel. But again and again the texts say God also intervened because God hated the oppression of the poor Israelites (Exod. 3:7–8; 6:5–7). Annually at the harvest festival the people of Israel repeated this confession: "The Egyptians mistreated us. . . . Then we cried out to the LORD, the God of our fathers, and the LORD heard our voice and saw our misery, toil and oppression. So the LORD brought us out of Egypt" (Deut. 26:6–8). God acts in history to lift up the poor and oppressed.

2. The Bible also teaches a second, more disturbing truth. *Sometimes, the Lord of history tears down rich and powerful people.* Mary's song is shocking: "My soul glorifies the Lord . . . He has filled the hungry with good things but has sent the rich away empty" (Luke 1:46, 53). James is even more nasty: "Now listen, you rich people, weep and wail because of the misery that is coming upon you" (James 5:1).

What is going on? Is creating wealth a bad thing? No. The Bible is very clear that God has created a gorgeous world and placed human beings in it to revel in its splendor and produce an abundance of good things. Is God biased? No. The Bible explicitly declares that God has no bias either toward the rich or the poor (Deut. 10:17–18).

What then is the problem? Why do the Scriptures warn again and again that God sometimes works in history to destroy the rich? The Bible has a simple answer. It is because the rich sometimes get rich by oppressing the poor. Or because they have plenty and neglect the needy. In either case, God is furious.

James warned the rich so harshly because they had hoarded wealth and refused to pay their workers (5:2–6). Repeatedly, the prophets said the same thing (Ps. 10; Isa.

3:14–25; Jer. 22:13–19). "Among my people are wicked men who lie in wait like men who snare birds and like those who set traps to catch men. Like cages full of birds, their houses are full of deceit; they have become rich and powerful and have grown fat and sleek.... They do not defend the rights of the poor. Should I not punish them for this?" (Jer. 5:26–29).

Repeatedly, the prophets warned that God was so outraged that he would destroy the nations of Israel and Judah. Because of the way they "trample on the heads of the poor ... and deny justice to the oppressed," Amos predicted terrible captivity (2:7; 5:11; 6:4, 7; 7:11, 17). So did Isaiah and Micah (Isa. 10:1–3; Micah 2:2; 3:12). And it happened just as they foretold. According to both the Old and New Testaments, God destroys people and societies that get rich by oppression.

But what if we work hard and create wealth in just ways? That is good and God is pleased—as long as we do not forget to share. No matter how justly we have acquired our wealth, God demands that we act generously toward the poor. When we do not, the Bible says, God treats us the same way he does those who oppress the poor. There is not a hint in Jesus' story of the rich man and Lazarus that the rich man exploited Lazarus to acquire wealth. He simply neglected to share. So God punished him (Luke 16:19–31).

Ezekiel contains a striking explanation for the destruction of Sodom: "Now this was the sin of your sister Sodom: She and her daughters were arrogant, overfed and unconcerned; they did not help the poor and needy.... Therefore I did away with them as you have seen" (16:49–50).

Again, the text does not charge them with gaining wealth by oppression. It was because they refused to share their abundance that God destroyed the city.

The Bible is clear. If we get rich by oppression or if we have wealth and do not reach out generously to the poor, the Lord acts in history to destroy us. God judges societies by what they do to the people at the bottom. That is how much God cares for the poor.

3. The next biblical truth about the poor is this: *The Bible says that God identifies with the poor so strongly that caring for them is almost like helping God.* "He who is kind to the poor lends to the LORD" (Prov. 19:17). Vinay and Colleen Samuel are making loans to the Creator of the universe! On the other hand, one "who oppresses the poor shows contempt for their Maker" (14:31).

Jesus' parable of the sheep and goats is the ultimate commentary on these two proverbs. Jesus surprises those on the right with his insistence that they had fed and clothed him when he was cold and hungry. When they protested that they could not remember ever doing that, Jesus replied: "Whatever you did for one of the least of these brothers of mine, you did for me" (Matt. 25:40). If we believe his words, we look on the poor and neglected with entirely new eyes.

4. Finally, *the Scriptures teach that God's faithful people share God's special concern for the poor.* God commanded Israel not to treat widows, orphans, and foreigners the way the Egyptians had treated them (Exod. 22:21–24). Instead, they should love the poor just as God cared for them at the Exodus (Exod. 22:21–24; Deut. 15:13–15). When Jesus' disciples throw parties, they should especially invite the poor and disabled (Luke 14:12–14; Heb. 13:1–3). Paul held up Jesus' model of becoming poor to show how generously the Corinthians should contribute to the poor in Jerusalem (2 Cor. 8:9).

The Bible, however, goes one shocking step further. God insists that if we do not imitate his concern for the poor we are not really his people–no matter how frequent our worship or how orthodox our creeds. Because Israel failed to correct oppression and defend poor widows, Isaiah insisted that Israel was really the pagan people of Gomorrah (1:10–17). God despised their fasting because they tried to worship God and oppress their workers at the same time (Isa. 58:3–7). Through Amos, the Lord shouted in fury that the very religious festivals he had ordained made him angry and sick. Why? Because the rich and powerful were mixing worship and oppression of the poor (5:21–24). Jesus was even more harsh. At the Last Judgment, some who expect to enter heaven will learn that their failure to feed the hungry condemns them to hell (Matt. 25). If we do not care for the needy brother or sister, we simply do not know God (1 John 3:17).

Jeremiah 22:13–19 is a most astonishing passage. Good king Josiah had a wicked son Jehoiakim. When Jehoiakim became king, he built a fabulous palace by oppressing his workers. God sent the prophet Jeremiah to announce a terrible punishment.

The most interesting part of the passage, however, is a short aside on this evil king's good father: "He defended the cause of the poor and needy, and so all went well. *'Is that not what it means to know me?'* declares the LORD" (v. 16, emphasis added). Knowing God is *inseparable* from caring for the poor. Of course, we dare not reduce knowing God only to a concern for the needy as some radical theologians do. We meet God in prayer, Bible study, worship–in many ways. But if we do not share God's passion to strengthen the poor, we simply do not know God in a biblical way.

I fear that many Christians today who think they are very orthodox are actually heretical at just this point. If Jeremiah 22:16 and 1 John 3:17 present one biblical criterion of genuine knowledge of God, what does God think about rich Christians who are living in countries that are sixty times as wealthy as the poorest one-fifth of the world's countries, and yet share less than 3 percent of their abundance? Is that not heretical defiance of explicit biblical teaching? As we Christians examine our houses, cars, and family budgets, can we say our lifestyles are conformed to Christ rather than the world?

Now please do not misunderstand me. I am not advocating poverty–or Marxism. I think creating wealth in just, sustainable ways is very good and urgently important. The unemployed need jobs. The Creator wants us to revel in the good earth given to us as a gift to treasure and develop.

The biblical teaching on poverty and possessions contains a wonderful subtlety and balance. There is a materialism that is godly. According to the Scriptures, the material world is not an illusion to ignore or an evil to escape. It is a good gift to embrace. It is a ring from our Beloved. The material world is so good that the Creator becomes flesh, so good that we await the resurrection of the body, so good that all creation stands on tiptoe eagerly anticipating the restoration of the groaning creation.

The Creator placed men and women in this fabulous world as stewards, uniquely shaped in the divine image to tend and care for God's good garden. Tracing the steps of the Creator in science, technology, and the responsible production of more wealth is very good. Christians should rejoice in the way the modern world has been able to produce such an abundance that it would be possible–if we cared enough–for every person living today to have the opportunity for quality education and good health care– not to mention enough food, clothing, and housing.

The Bible, however, also issues a warning at just this point. Material abundance acquired justly is a good gift. But it is also dangerous. It is so easy to trust in our wealth rather than God (1 Tim. 6:9–10). It is so easy to treasure material things more than persons and God. We cannot serve God and mammon (Matt. 6:24). Strangely, growing wealth often hardens our hearts to the poor rather than sparking greater generosity.

A recent study of Christian giving illustrates the problem.[7] In 1968 per capita income in the United States was $9,831 and church members on average gave 3.14 percent. By 1992, per capita income had grown to $14,515 (in constant 1987 dollars). But we only gave 2.52 percent! It is so easy to imitate the rich fool preoccupied with constructing ever larger barns (Luke 12:16–21) rather than the good wife of Proverbs who "opens her arms to the poor" (31:20).

Our world desperately needs a biblically balanced understanding of wealth. And also poverty! Some people want to blame the victims for their poverty. Don't the poor create their own misery by laziness and sinful choices about sex and alcohol? Others think a wicked "system" is entirely to blame. The real world is far more complex.

Some people are poor because they make sinful choices. Others are poor because they believe a religious worldview that denies them dignity and discourages change. (Hinduism's caste system, for example, claims that both the rich and the poor should accept their fate so they will be better off in a future reincarnation.) In both situations, people need to hear the gospel, embrace a biblical worldview about the dignity of all, and experience the redeeming power of Christ.

Some people are poor because of natural disasters or inadequate tools and knowledge. They need Christians who will share emergency food and appropriate technology so they can produce enough to care for their families.

Still others are poor because of injustice in the way the courts work, the laws are made, the land has been divided, or opportunities for education and jobs are shared. Earlier we saw the very explicit biblical teaching that sometimes people get rich by oppressing others. Christians need to work with all people of goodwill to create free, just social systems. God wants everyone to have the opportunity to own property and earn a living that enables them to participate freely as dignified members of their community.[8]

Biblical people know that bread and justice for everyone is very important. They also know it is not enough. The poor of the world also need Jesus. They need to know that no matter how despised, trampled, and famished, the Creator of the world loves them so much that Jesus would gladly have died just for them. They need to know that right now, the risen Lord longs to forgive their sins, transform their broken lives, and welcome them to life eternal. They also need to know that this same God cares especially for the poor, hates injustice, and now invites them to become coworkers in transforming society.

Think of what would happen if we shared this full biblical message with the more than one billion people who do not know either justice or Jesus. Of course, they won't believe us unless we preach Good News to the poor the way Jesus did. He lived what he preached. He walked with the poor and met their material needs as he taught and preached. Think of the explosive power that would flow from a church today living as he lived. The poor of Jesus' day never doubted that bringing Good News to the poor (Luke 4:18) was one central part of his mission. All they needed to do was look at what he said and did. But when today's poor look at the church, they have strong reasons for doubting that we are serious about Jesus. Unless Christians today live sharing lifestyles that match God's concern for the poor, our preaching will be weak and our faith heretical.

What would it take for Christians today to convince the poor that we are truly disciples of Jesus?

Many more would have to join Vinay and Colleen Samuel, and move from the suburbs to the slums, from the chair to the floor. Even more would need to become partners with those who move by sharing our money and our prayers. It would be a costly discipleship. But the results would be amazing.

The story of David Bussau points to what could happen. David started out as an orphan. He still does not know anything about his parents. But he learned of God's love at the orphanage where he lived until he was seventeen. When he left, he discovered that God had given him very unusual business skills. Virtually every business he tried prospered. David made his first million by the time he was thirty-five.

Then God began to sensitize him to the needs of the poor. He and his wife, Carol, increasingly felt, he says, that the Holy Spirit was calling them to use their skills and resources "for the sake of the kingdom and not just for the sake of making a profit." In 1976, the whole family moved to a desperately poor Christian village in Bali, Indonesia. Over the next few years, David discovered the amazing way that tiny loans to very poor people can slowly transform their lives. Banks had no interest in making micro-loans of $25, $50, or $200 to tiny entrepreneurs with no experience or collateral. David, however, discovered that small loans plus a little technical assistance worked wonders. Suddenly, a poor person could purchase some simple tools or enough supplies to increase the family's income. They gladly paid the money back at a fair interest rate.

These small loans began to make a difference in the lives of desperate people like Riasa, who lives in Indonesia. Riasa is a disabled widow with two dependents living in a society with no disability pension, no health benefits, and no unemployment benefits. Her small house with a thatched roof has no electricity, no running water, no toilet—just a mud floor. She has to care for a seven-year-old daughter and an aged mother-in-law. Polio deformed her right arm and leg. But Riasa has hope because of loans from one of David's partners. With her first loan of twenty-five dollars (U.S.) she bought corn and made small cakes to sell in the local market. From the profits she repaid that loan and then expanded her tiny business with a second fifty-dollar loan. Now repaying her third loan, she plans to open a small shop at the front of her tiny house.

In the early eighties, the Protestant Church of Bali asked David to develop a large micro-loan program. They make loans to both Christians and Hindus. In fact, over 85 percent of the loans have gone to Hindus. But the program has a clear evangelistic intention. An interview with the local Christian pastor is the first step for anyone seeking a loan. From 1983–1991, this church program in Bali made about nine thousand loans and created over twenty-two thousand new jobs.

The result has been a great blessing to the Bali church. The loan program has helped the Bali church become largely self-supporting. In 1975, the entire Bali Protestant Church had only nineteen pastors and 90 percent of their support came from the West. By 1991, there were 48 pastors and 85 percent of their support came from the local congregations. The number of Bali Christians has grown by 300 to 400 percent in the last thirty years. Micro-loans have had a dramatic impact.

This program of micro-loans to the poor in the name of Jesus has spread rapidly. Today, David Bussau and his partners in the Opportunity Network make micro-loans in dozens of developing countries in Asia, Africa, and Latin America. Donor networks are also springing up in many industrialized nations. From 1981–1993, Opportunity made forty-six thousand loans and created seventy-eight thousand jobs among the poor. Typically, each loan helps a family of five. Within a year, they repay the loan–and enjoy a 50 percent increase in their family income! David and his partners have changed the lives of many hundreds of thousands of people.[9]

Think of what would happen if large numbers of Christians caught the vision. Christians today have an annual income of about ten trillion dollars.[10] Hardly any of us would slip into poverty if we decided to give a tithe (10 percent) of that income instead of the typical 2.5 percent to charity. Let's suppose that just 10 percent of the Christians (with an annual income of one trillion dollars) decided to tithe. Ten percent of one trillion is one hundred billion dollars. Let's assume we give half of that to our local churches. Then let's suppose we give the other half for a little while to the kind of micro-loans among the poor that David Bussau makes. What would happen?

David tells me that $500 is enough to cover all the costs for a loan that will impact a family of five and increase their income by 50 percent within a year. How many loans would fifty billion dollars make? One hundred million loans! Each loan impacts a family of five, so fifty billion dollars and one hundred million loans would dramatically improve the lives of five hundred million poor people! In two years, we could provide two hundred million loans to empower one billion people—which is a large percentage of the total number of people estimated to be desperately poor today. A mere 10 percent of today's Christians could improve the life of all the world's poorest one billion people by 50 percent in just two years—if we would only be willing to share a mere 5 percent (just half a tithe) of our income.

Undoubtedly, if we really started to do this, there would be unexpected problems. The efficiency ratio might drop. I don't pretend that the above sketch is a precise business plan. But however much the calculation may need refining, one thing is wonderfully clear. We have the money to produce fantastic improvement! Without falling into poverty, Christians today could dramatically transform the lives of the poorest one-fifth of our neighbors.

Now is the time to multiply a thousandfold Christian work in micro-loans to the poor. Gladly we should loan to people of every religion. But always in the name of Jesus and always with the prayer and longing for the right opportunity to share the gospel in a sensitive, nonmanipulative way. People need both jobs and Jesus. It may be that micro-loans and micro-enterprise development will be to missions in the twenty-first century what education and medicine were in the last two centuries.

The idea is catching on. At an international conference on Christian faith and economics, the Agra Covenant on

Christian Capital was written. A growing number of Christians are signing the covenant and pledging to give 1 percent of the current year's income to small loans for the poor.[11]

Obviously micro-loans by themselves cannot solve all problems. People need good schools, health care, and many other things besides a loan. That is why Vinay and Colleen Samuel operate their many-sided program that cares for the whole person. But micro-loans done in cooperation with David Bussau is one of their favorite ministries, because it empowers the poor to help themselves.

Think of how two hundred million loans in the name of Christ would change the world. We have the money and we know what works. Do we have the faith and obedience? Are enough people ready to move from the chair to the floor? Are enough people ready to support them with prayers and funds?

If we did that in the name of Jesus, the impact would be stunning. Skeptics would reconsider Christianity. Revival would break out. Untold numbers would come to Christ. Church planting would accelerate. Global tensions would decrease. The One who is both Creator and Redeemer would rejoice.

If Christians today–even just a fraction of us–truly implement God's concern for the poor, the world will change.

10

TENDING THE GARDEN WITHOUT WORSHIPING IT

Characteristic Ten

Genuine Christians treasure the creation and worship the Creator

Some Christians think environmentalists are New Age pagans who worship trees and belittle people. Some environmentalists think Christians at best have no concern for the environment and at worst want to use it all up fast because they think God will blow it all to bits at the Second Coming. Neither group has met Larry Schweiger.

Larry is a devout Christian and a dedicated environmentalist. For years, he was a senior vice president at the National Wildlife Federation, a large, five-million-member secular environmental organization.

Recently, Larry told me about the spiritual longing he has found among many environmentalists, who sense the need for a deeper religious foundation for their passionate care for the earth. Tragically, many of them think that Christianity is the problem instead of the answer. But many are open when Larry shares a full-orbed biblical perspective. In fact, in recent years Larry has led two weekly

Bible studies for about forty staff members at the National Wildlife Federation. Larry has also had the joy of leading several people there to personal faith in Christ.

Larry believes that biblical faith provides the best foundation for caring for the creation entrusted to us by the Creator, and it pains him when some Christians dismiss concern for creation as a New Age plot or an attack on free enterprise. Larry treasures streams, flowers, birds, and trees because he loves and worships the One who made them.

In recent years, Larry has felt God calling him to focus his energy in two areas. He wants to show secular environmentalists the solid, spiritual foundation they long for. And he prays for opportunities to help biblical Christians better understand that the Bible summons them to loving care for the gorgeous garden God has placed in their hands.

More and more devout Christians are urging a new concern for the creation. Scores of evangelical leaders recently endorsed the "Evangelical Declaration on the Care of Creation."[1]

Billy Graham has confessed: "I find myself becoming more and more an advocate for the true ecologists. . . . Many of these people have done us an essential service in helping us preserve and protect our green zones and our cities, our water and our air."[2]

Graham tells the story of his beloved Sugar Creek, which ran through the middle of his father's farm. One morning, he found a cow lying dead by the stream. A mill upstream was dumping deadly poison into the water. "We couldn't do anything then," Graham continues. "There were no laws to which my father could appeal to have Sugar Creek cleaned and restored."[3] All Billy Graham's dad could do back then was build a fence so the cattle could not drink the poisoned water.

Christians who think carefully about the environment discover a big problem—in fact three problems. Environmental degradation is not a silly fiction created by mad scientists and political demagogues. The world's rivers, lakes, and air *are* polluted. There *are* dangerous holes in the ozone layer. Carbon dioxide emissions from our cars and factories threaten global warming that could raise ocean levels, produce drastic changes in the climate, and flood some of our great coastal cities. In the last forty years, we have lost one-third of our rain forests. We face serious environmental danger.[4]

But we also have another problem: Some people most concerned about these dangers insist that historic Christianity is the problem. We must, they tell us, reject the biblical teachings that the Creator is distinct from the earth and that people alone are made in the image of God. Actress Shirley MacLaine tells us that we must become Eastern monists and believe that you and I are gods. Others tell us to worship the goddess, Mother Earth. Radical theologian Matthew Fox tells us that we should turn away from a theology that talks about sin, grace, and redemption, and in its place, we should substitute "creation spirituality" with nature, rather than the Bible, as our primary revelation. Australian scientist Peter Singer says that people are no more important than monkeys and mosquitoes. To think that we are more valuable is to fall into the terrible error of "speciesism." Singer even thinks the primates ought to have their own separate "nation-state" called "Gorillastan."

Fortunately, biblical Christians reject this theological nonsense. But then so often we turn around and worship the earth in a different way. By the cars we drive, the houses we purchase, and the affluent lifestyles we live, our lives show that we really worship the god of materialistic consumerism—which is our third problem.

Christians today urgently need to come to love God's creation in a far deeper way. Christians must care for creation because God's Word demands it; because we are destroying the Creator's garden; because we are endangering a decent life for our grandchildren and their grandchildren; and because many secular environmentalists are on an intense spiritual pilgrimage, and if we don't show them that biblical faith is what they are looking for, they will find some other religious foundation for their ecological concerns.

Make no mistake: A spiritual battle is raging. Satan would love nothing better than to persuade modern people that the best way to solve our environmental crisis is to abandon historic Christian truth. The way to defeat this demonic lie is for all Christians to become committed environmentalists and to ground their struggle to care for creation on solid biblical foundations.

But are the planet's biological systems—which are essential for human life—really in danger? Do scientists believe there is a serious problem? The answer is yes. It is true that some irresponsible people have exaggerated the danger. It is also true that others point to the substantial progress in reducing pollution of air and water made by wealthy nations and argue that there is no environmental crisis. However, we must listen to careful scientists, not apocalyptic doomsayers or naive optimists.

What do these responsible scientists say? They are worried. A majority of all living recipients of the Nobel Prize in the sciences recently signed the "World Scientists' Warning to Humanity."[5] Together 104 Nobel laureates plus more than 1,500 prominent scientists from more than seventy countries pleaded with us to reduce our pollution and end our overconsumption before the dangers become irreversible. "No more than one or a few decades remain," they warn, "before the chance to avert the threats we now confront will be lost and the prospects for humanity immeasurably diminished."

What is causing these problems? We overfish our seas, pollute our atmosphere, exhaust our supplies of fresh water, and destroy precious topsoil, forests, and unique species lovingly shaped by the Creator. In many countries, chemicals, pesticides, oil spills, and industrial emissions degrade air, water, and soil. "Is it not enough for you to feed on the good pasture?" the Creator asks in the Bible. "Must you also trample the rest of your pasture with your feet? Is it not enough for you to drink clear water? Must you also muddy the rest with your feet?" (Ezek. 34:18).

Dramatic headlines about the rapid decline of commercial fishing off the east cost of the United States and Canada underscore the dangerous global trend. All the world's seventeen major oceanic fishing areas are now being fished at or above capacity.[6] Russia's Aral Sea used to yield forty-four thousand tons of fish a year. Today all the fish are dead. Why? Because massive irrigation projects raised the salt content to a deadly level.[7] From 1989 to 1994, the global fish catch per person declined 8 percent.

We are also degrading the atmosphere that we need to live. Man-made chemicals have destroyed parts of the upper atmosphere's ozone layer, which protects people, animals, and plants from the sun's deadly ultraviolet radiation. North Americans have reduced air pollution in many cities, but rapidly worsening pollution is increasing disease and death in many cities in developing nations.

Scientists debate the extent of global warming. But carbon dioxide (given off when we burn fossil fuels and trees) and other "greenhouse" gases produce a greenhouse effect because they let the sun's heat enter our atmosphere, but then trap it here. (The process is similar to what happens when the glass walls of a greenhouse let in the sun's heat and then prevent that heat from radiating back into the sky.) In 1992, an international panel of leading climate scientists from twenty-two countries concluded that if we do not reduce our production of greenhouse gases, global temperatures may rise by 3° to 8° Fahrenheit (the earth has warmed by only 5° to 9° since the coldest period of the last ice age).[8] The result would be rising sea levels, the flooding of coastal cities, and dramatic changes in global climate. In late 1995, the Intergovernmental Panel on Climate Change reported that global warming had begun.

In many parts of the world, we are degrading or destroying the soil that produces our food. Since 1945, an area of land covered by vegetation larger than India and China has been degraded.[9] The United States has four hundred million acres of cropland. Every year, we pave over, build on, or somehow convert to urban use 3 million acres of this precious soil. Over much of what was formerly prairie land, we lose two bushels of topsoil for every bushel of corn grown.[10]

Tropical forests provide a home to a majority of the world's living species. They also convert vast amounts of carbon dioxide into the oxygen we must have to breath. Foolishly, we are destroying these forests much faster than we are replacing them. Every year an area the size of the state of Indiana disappears.[11] At present rates, most of the tropical forests will be gone in one hundred years.[12]

One-half of all U.S. medicines come from genetic material from wild plants found mostly in tropical forests. But we are destroying these forests and the unique species they protect at a ferocious pace. World famous botanist and evangelical Christian Ghillean Prance predicts that at current rates more than one million different kinds of animals, insects, and plants will become extinct by the year 2000.[13] In the "World Scientists' Warning to Humanity," the scientists suggest that one-third of all species existing today may be lost by the year 2100. Unlike human beings, plants and animals are not made in the image of God. We rightly use them to make life more healthy and wholesome. But dare we wantonly, unnecessarily destroy millions of unique species that the Creator carefully, lovingly created? Ezekiel's words are for us: "Is it not enough for you to feed on the good pasture? Must you also trample the rest of your pasture with your feet?" (Ezek. 34:18).

Is it any wonder that today's best scientists are concerned? As they carefully study what is happening to the environment, they feel compelled to warn us of danger and plead with us to change the way we live: "A great change in our stewardship of the earth and the life on it is required if vast human misery is to be avoided and our global home on this planet is not to be irretrievably mutilated." At the end of the "World Scientists' Warning to Humanity," these distinguished scientists urge the religious community to help. I have personally talked about this problem with prominent scientists like Carl Sagan and Henry Kendall. Sagan does not hide his unbelief. But he eagerly invites religious people to help reduce the danger to the earth. Secular scientists are pleading with Christians to take better care of God's creation!

If we listen, we will hear the same message coming from the Bible. Four biblical principles are especially important if we are to care for creation as faithful stewards.

First, we must hold together God's transcendence and God's immanence. God is different from creation. God transcends everything created. But the God who is omnipresent is also in creation. If we focus only on God's immanence (his presence in the world), we land in pantheism where everything is divine and good as it is. If we talk only about God's transcendence (his radical separateness from creation), we miss God's continuing love for and involvement with everything God created.

The biblical God is both immanent and transcendent. He is not a cosmic watchmaker who wound up the global clock and then abandoned it to run on its own. He continues to work in the creation. In Job we read that God gives orders to the morning (38:12), that the eagle soars at his commands (39:27), and that he provides food for the ravens when their young cry out in hunger (38:41). The Creator, however, is also radically distinct from creation. Creation is finite, limited, dependent; the Creator is infinite, unlimited, self-sufficient.

Second, human beings are both interdependent with the rest of creation and unique within it. Sometimes we Christians forget how tightly our lives are interlocked with the rest of creation. Our daily physical existence depends on the forests, oceans, and grasslands. Everything is interrelated in the global ecosystem. The emissions from our cars contribute to the destruction of trees—trees that convert the carbon dioxide we breathe out into the oxygen we need to breathe in. Christians today must recover an appreciation of our dependence on the trees and flowers, the streams and forests. Unless we do, we shall surely perish. Or at least our children and grandchildren will miss the joy of living in a safe, healthy, and beautiful environment.

The Bible, however, also insists on two other things about humanity. Human beings *alone* are created in the image of God. And we *alone* have been given a special "dominion" or stewardship. It is a biblical truth, not speciesism, to say that only human beings—and not trees and animals—are created in the image of God (Gen. 1:27). This truth is the foundation of our God-given mandate to care for ("have stewardship over") the nonhuman creation (Gen. 1:28; Ps. 8).

If our status is no different from that of animals and plants, we cannot eat them for food or use them to build civilizations. We do *not* need to apologize to brother carrot when we have lunch. We are free to use the resources of the earth for human purposes. Created in the divine image, we alone have been placed in charge of the earth. At the same time, our dominion must be the gentle care of a loving gardener, not the callous exploitation of a self-centered lord. So we should not wipe out species or waste the nonhuman creation. Only a careful, stewardly use of God's plants and animals is legitimate for human beings who worship the Creator.

Tragically—and arrogantly—we have distorted dominion into domination. A famous essay by writer Lynn White correctly placed some blame for environmental decay on Christianity.[14] But it is a misunderstanding of the Bible, not God's Word itself, that is at fault.

Genesis 2:15 says the Lord put us in the garden "to work it and take care of it." The word translated work is the Hebrew word *abad*, and it means "to serve." The related noun actually means "slave" or "servant." The word translated "take care of" is the Hebrew word *shamar*, which suggests watchful care and preservation. The Bible calls us to serve and watch lovingly over God's good garden, not rape it.

The second biblical principle, then, is that although human beings do have a unique status in creation, we are also very interdependent with the rest of creation.

Third, we need a God-centered, rather than a human-centered, worldview. That is important in order to respect the independent worth of the nonhuman creation. Christians have too easily and too often fallen into the trap of supposing that the nonhuman creation has worth only as it serves human purposes. This is not what the Bible teaches.

Genesis 1 makes clear that all creation is good–good, according to the Bible, even before human beings arrived on the scene. Colossians 1:16 reveals that all things are created for Christ. It doesn't say they are created for you and me, although that's also true. This text says the creation was made for Christ! According to Job 39:1–2, God watches over the doe in the mountains. No human being may ever see her. But God counts the months of her pregnancy and gently watches over her when she gives birth! The first purpose of the nonhuman creation, then, is to glorify God, not to serve us.

Creation is part of God's revelation to us. "The heavens are telling the glory of God; and the firmament proclaims his handiwork. Day to day pours forth speech, and night to night declares knowledge. There is no speech, nor are there words; their voice is not heard; yet their voice goes out through all the earth, and their words to the end of the world" (Ps. 19:1–4 RSV).

One striking biblical teaching is that God has a covenant, not only with persons, but also with the nonhuman creation.

Did you realize that after the flood, God made a covenant with the *animals* as well as with Noah? "Behold, I establish my covenant with you and your descendants after you, *and* with every living creature that is with you, the birds, the cattle, and every beast of the earth with you, as many as came out of the ark" (Gen. 9:9–10 RSV, emphasis added).

Jesus recognized God's covenant with the whole of creation when he marveled over the way God feeds the birds and clothes the lilies (Matt. 6:26–30). The nonhuman creation has its own worth and dignity apart from its service to humanity.

Insisting on the independent dignity of the nonhuman creation does not mean that we ignore the biblical teaching that it has been given to human beings for our stewardship and use. But always our use of the nonhuman creation must be a thoughtful stewardship that honors the creation's independent dignity and worth in the eyes of the Creator.

Finally, God's cosmic plan of redemption includes the nonhuman creation. This truth provides a crucial foundation for building a Christian theology for an environmental age. Romans 8:19–23 shows that the whole created order, including the material world of bodies and rivers and trees, will be part of the heavenly kingdom. That truth confirms that the created order is good and important.

The Bible's affirmation of the material world can be seen most clearly in Christ himself. Not only did the Creator enter his creation by becoming flesh and blood to redeem us from our sin. The God-man was also resurrected *bodily* from the tomb.

The goodness of the created order is also revealed in how the Bible describes the coming kingdom. Apparently the language of feasting and banqueting is necessary to describe our glorious future! We will sit down at the "wedding supper of the Lamb" (Rev. 19:9). The material world is so good that even when we think of Christ's return, we rightly think of feasting on bread, wine, and all the glorious fruit of the earth.

Eastern monists think the created order is an illusion to escape. Biblical people know that the creation is in itself so good that God is going to purge it of the evil introduced by the fall and restore it to wholeness. Romans 8 tells us that at Christ's return, when we experience the resurrection of the body, then the groaning creation will be transformed: "The creation itself will be liberated from its bondage to decay and brought into the glorious freedom of the children of God" (v. 21).

I live near the Schuylkill River in Philadelphia. It is a lovely river, but it is badly polluted. You can catch fish there but you can't eat them. I rejoice in the divine promise of Romans 8 that the returning Christ will restore even the groaning creation to wholeness. In Christ's coming kingdom, I hope to go sailing on an unpolluted Schuylkill River with my grandchildren.

We need a theology both of creation and of redemption. The Christian hope for Christ's return must be joined with our doctrine of creation. Knowing that we are summoned by the Creator to be wise gardeners caring for God's good earth, knowing the biblical hope that someday the earth will be restored, genuine Christians should take the lead in caring for our lovely, endangered earthly home.

That means we must repent of our overconsumption and materialism. That means more than recycling bottles or newspapers although that is a good place to start. Many Christians have become materialistic consumers just like their neighbors. We need to repent of our unspoken belief that more is better, that more and more material abundance automatically brings greater fulfillment. Would it not be hypocritical and ironic if biblical people condemned New Age environmentalists for their worship of the earth and then continue rushing madly down their present path of ever increasing idolatrous consumerism?

Precisely as we think about what to do to care for the earth, one thing is very striking. Many of the things to be done are identical with the things we need to do to feed the hungry and empower the poor. At least fifty thousand people die each day of starvation, malnutrition, and related diseases. One-fifth of the world's people live near absolute poverty. We must live more simply so that others may simply live. If we reduce our affluent lifestyles, we can share more with the poor and place less strain on the environment.

It is not that the earth lacks the resources to feed everyone. Nor is it that providing a decent life for all would destroy the environment. But if the rich and powerful insist on an ever escalating accumulation of material things for themselves, then we cannot overcome poverty and preserve a sustainable environment.

Do we really want to pollute our land, air, and water and destroy untold species of birds, plants, and animals lovingly shaped by the Creator just to increase our affluence? That is not to argue that spotted owls are of equal value with persons. If we must choose between destroying a species of birds or driving people into poverty and starvation, biblical people will value persons more than birds. But very seldom if ever do we face only those two harsh alternatives. We are polluting the earth and destroying species to feed our ever growing materialism.

That is not to call for poverty or asceticism. There is a powerful, wonderful materialism in the Bible. It is different from materialistic consumerism, different from Marxist philosophical materialism, and different from worship of the earth. But it is certainly a kind of materialism.

We have seen that the material world is so good that the One who created all things and pronounced them very good actually became flesh. The material world is so good that Jesus rose *bodily* from the tomb. The material world is so good that all believers will be resurrected bodily to dance and revel in a renewed creation when the Lord returns. That's how good the material world is. It is hardly surprising that God wants you and me to rejoice now in the good earth's bounty.

But there is another side to the biblical teaching. Nothing in the world, not even the whole world, is worth as much as our soul, as our relationship with Jesus Christ. The one who loved to bless wedding feasts calls us to be ready to forsake wife, husband, father, mother, houses, and lands for the sake of his kingdom. Nothing, absolutely nothing, not even everything in the whole world, is as important as a living relationship with Jesus Christ, which leads to life eternal.

Centuries ago, the great Christian theologian from North Africa, St. Augustine, captured this biblical perspective with his lovely image of the ring and the Beloved. The material world is a gorgeous ring given to humanity by the Divine Lover. The Beloved wants us to enjoy its splendor. Surely however, it is absurdly foolish to focus our affection on the ring and forget the Beloved.

It is precisely this balanced biblical perspective that will help us avoid the destructive rat race of unbridled consumption. The planet cannot sustain ten billion people living the kind of ever-more affluent lifestyle North Americans now demand.

The Creator who made us both body and soul wants us to enjoy the gorgeous bounty of the material world. At the same time, we are created in such a way that human wholeness and fulfillment come not only from material things, but also from right relationships with neighbor and God. The call to care for the neighbor and the summons to sabbatical worship of God both place limits on human acquisition and consumption. Material things are very good, but less important than spending time with and enjoying right relationships with neighbor and God.

Modern materialism comes from the eighteenth-century Enlightenment, which abandoned this biblical worldview. The isolated, autonomous individual replaced God at the center of reality. The scientific method became the only avenue to truth and reality.

We can measure an ever increasing GNP and an expanding stock portfolio. We cannot easily measure the goodness of community in the extended family, or the value of caring for the neighbor–not to mention the value of a personal relationship with God. Frantically, each individual seeks fulfillment in more and more material things, even though our very nature makes it impossible for such things to satisfy our deepest needs. The destructive, unbridled consumerism of modern society is rooted in this narcissistic naturalism that flows from the Enlightenment. Biblical faith, on the other hand, provides a framework within which we can both enjoy material abundance and understand its limits.

If we turn from modern errors and return to the biblical view of creation, how should we change? A recent book by a good friend Calvin De Witt is full of helpful suggestions. Cal is a professor of environmental studies at the University of Wisconsin. He is also a devout Christian.

In *Earth-Wise*, De Witt invites each local congregation to become a biblical "Creation Awareness Center." God's love for creation can become a regular part of sermons, worship, Sunday School, and youth programs. An energy audit can save fossil fuels (and money). As caring for creation becomes a regular feature of church life, individuals and families will turn away from their destructive lifestyles of overconsumption. Whole neighborhoods will blossom anew as congregational Creation Awareness Communities lead their neighbors in new programs to preserve the environment. *Earth-Wise* is biblical, easy to read, and full of scores of practical suggestions. The same is true of the biblical environmental magazine *Creation Care* published by the Evangelical Environmental Network.[15]

We can make a difference. Think of the impact if faithful Christians today would become devoted environmentalists. Think of the impact if biblical people would take the lead to reduce pollution, save endangered species, and avoid ecological disaster. We would leave a better world for our grandchildren and their grandchildren. Most important, we would honor the Creator.

We might also discover unexpected evangelistic opportunities. An evangelical university group at Indiana University is working with my organization Green Cross to develop a major emphasis on care for creation in their campus work. Why? Obviously they want to be obedient and tend the Creator's garden. But they also know that many non-Christian students on campus are dedicated environmentalists. They believe that if they as biblical Christians become known as people who care deeply about creation, that will open many doors for sharing their faith.

First Presbyterian Church in Mt. Holly, New Jersey, has developed a similar program. From time to time, they develop evangelistic services for unchurched people by focusing on "hot" issues like racism and the environment. For the evangelistic service on the environment, they wrote a popular tract called "Recruiting for a Renewed Earth." The prayer written for those invited to accept Christ at the service ends with the words: "I want to be part of your plan for the children of God and your renewed creation."

Faithful Christians today will carefully tend the Creator's garden. We will revel in its astonishing splendor and awesome glory. But we will worship only the Creator who is also the Redeemer. We will fall at Jesus' feet in breathless adoration and total surrender, thanking our Beloved for the gorgeous ring he has given us to enjoy. But we will always remember that the Beloved himself is more precious than all the gems on all the billions of spinning galaxies.

CONCLUSION

CHRISTIAN FAITH AS SERVANTHOOD

Characteristic Eleven

Genuine Christians embrace servanthood

What is the first thing that comes to mind when the gay community in Grand Rapids thinks about Jerry Falwell's former vice president? A *Christianity Today* headline tells the story: "Ed Dobson loves homosexuals."

Dobson has pastored the largest evangelical church in Grand Rapids since 1987. Dobson considers homosexual practice sin, and he clearly teaches the biblical truth that God wants sex to be reserved for a man and woman united in lifelong marriage covenant. He is opposed to the radical gay political agenda.

Why then the *Christianity Today* headline? It all started when a grieving mother wrote and asked Reverend Dobson to visit her sick son. She was afraid Jim had AIDS. Jim had grown up at Calvary Church–the church that Dobson pastors. Years ago, Jim had left the church and joined the gay community.

Dobson's first visit with Jim in the hospital happened to be the very day the doctors told him that he had AIDS. Jim was terrified and talked for a long time with Dobson. After praying with Jim, Dobson left a copy of Billy Graham's *Peace with God.* When Dobson returned the next day, Jim eagerly reported that he had read the booklet and accepted Christ. Dobson and Calvary Church walked with Jim, day by day, until he died five years later.

As he worked with Jim, Ed Dobson sensed a call to serve other people with AIDS. "One question haunted me. What would Jesus do?"[1] Dobson decided to visit the local AIDS Resource Center. The director was shocked that the pastor of the largest evangelical church in the city cared about people with AIDS.

Slowly, Calvary developed ways of serving people with AIDS. For instance, a church member is now on the board of the AIDS Resource Center. The church buys Christmas presents for families affected by AIDS, and the church pays the funeral expenses of anyone who dies with AIDS and has no money for the funeral. And Calvary's chapel is available–at no cost–for the funeral service.

It has not always been an easy journey. Hate letters poured in the week after Dobson announced the church's new ministry to people with AIDS. One letter warned: "If you get involved with HIV/AIDS, this church will be overrun with homosexuals."

The next Sunday, Dobson responded, "If the church gets overrun with homosexuals, that will be terrific. They can take their place in the pews right next to the liars, gossips, materialists." At the end, Dobson declared, "When I die if someone stands up and says, 'Ed Dobson loved homosexuals,' then I will have accomplished something with my life."[2]

Perhaps the most astonishing development was an editorial in the local gay and lesbian newsletter. The writer explicitly noted that Calvary Church believes that "practicing gays, lesbians and bisexuals are practicing sin" but also thanked Calvary for inviting gays and lesbians to their services. Nobody in the homosexual community imagines that the church endorses their sinful lifestyle. But they know Ed Dobson and his church are gentle servants to people dying with AIDS.

Ed Dobson fears that "Christians are often better at hating than at loving." Why is it that the people who worship the Servant King are so seldom known as servants?

Why do most gay people think that evangelical Christians hate them? Why do many secular women fear and despise pro-life Christians? Why do so many women feel that Christian political engagement to restore family values represents a hostile threat to the equality of women? Why do people of other faiths frequently resent Christian evangelistic programs as cultural imperialism? How could it be that a national survey discovered that 34 percent of academics consider evangelical Christians a "threat to democracy" in the United States today?[3] Or that an editorial in the *New York Times* could warn that the political activity of religious conservatives "poses a far greater threat to democracy than was presented by Communism?"[4]

Part of the answer, of course, is that people get defensive when someone calls attention to their sin. Nor can we ignore the fact that secular elites dislike and fear the growing political influence of theologically conservative Christians. All that is true. But it is only one part of the explanation.

Too often Christians have failed to combine servanthood with truth. Too often we have been more ferocious in attacking sin than we are gentle in loving sinners. Too often our evangelism has come mixed with Western cultural arrogance and oppressive colonialism rather than immersed in acts of service and care. Too often our political engagement has been a self-serving demand for power rather than a servant voice for the poor and weak. Too often, we have failed to imitate our Servant King.

I remember a cartoon that mocked the renewed evangelical political activity in recent years. The cartoon alluded to early church history when Roman emperors fed Christians to the lions for the amusement of the pagan masses crowded into the Colosseum. In the cartoon, ferocious lions lunge at the defenseless victims. But the victims are labeled "liberals," not Christians. The announcer, pointing to the angry, devouring lions, says: "Check your program—*those* are the Christians!"

Whether or not such stereotypes are accurate and fair, they seriously undermine Christian credibility. What can be done?

Nothing is more important today than for Christians to recover genuine servanthood. People listened respectfully to Mother Teresa because they knew she was a servant. Imagine the impact if serving others was the first thing that came to mind when non-Christians thought of Christian televangelists or Christian politicians.

At the center of Christianity stands a Servant. "The heart of Christian faith—indeed the very object of Christian faith—is a Servant. This Servant is at the very center of the universe and is the object of our ultimate allegiance. 'Then I saw a Lamb, looking as if it had been slain, standing in the center of the throne' (Rev. 5:6)."[5]

Jesus insisted that he "did not come to be served, but to serve" (Mark 10:45). Both in life and death, he acted that way. He stooped to wash his disciples' feet. He spent vast amounts of time tenderly ministering to the physical needs of hurting people. He went out of his way to bring love and dignity to socially marginalized groups like lepers, tax collectors, bleeding women, blind beggars, and even a guilty adulteress.

Enduring Roman crucifixion in our place was his ultimate act of servanthood. Both Jesus and the early church understood the cross in light of Isaiah's suffering servant:

> Surely he took up our infirmities
>   and carried our sorrows. . . .
> But he was pierced for our transgressions,
>   he was crushed for our iniquities;
> the punishment that brought us peace was upon him,
>   and by his wounds we are healed.

Isaiah 53:4–5[6]

We fundamentally distort Jesus' gospel and Jesus' claims unless we see them coming from a humble servant. Jesus did claim to have divine authority to forgive sins. He did claim to be the unique Son of God. He did claim to be the long expected Messiah. He did dare to declare that no one can come to the Father but through him. But all of this he said as a humble servant tenderly ministering to lepers and prostitutes.

Jesus not only modeled servanthood, he commanded his disciples to follow in his steps. In Jesus' day, washing dusty feet was a degrading task left to slaves and social inferiors, but Jesus himself stooped to this lowly labor. After washing their feet, Jesus told his astonished disciples, "Now that I, your Lord and Teacher, have washed your feet, you also should wash one another's feet. I have set you an example that you should do as I have done for you" (John 13:14–15).

During his public ministry, Jesus demanded sacrificial servanthood of all who wanted to follow him. "If any want to become my followers, let them deny themselves and take up their cross and follow me" (Mark 8:34 NRSV). As he was about to leave his disciples and return to the Father, he commanded them to continue in the same servant-life fashion. "As the Father has sent me, I am sending you" (John 20:21).

It is hardly surprising that all through the rest of the New Testament, the apostles urge Christians to imitate Jesus' servanthood in every area of life. In the home, husbands must love their wives in the same costly way that "Christ loved the church and gave himself up for her" (Eph. 5:25). In the market place, Peter urged, Christians should remember even when mistreated, that "Christ suffered for you, leaving you an example, that you should follow in his steps" (1 Peter 2:21). In the church above all, Jesus is the model of humility and service: "Your attitude should be the same as that of Christ Jesus: Who, being in very nature God, . . . made himself nothing, taking the very nature of a servant" (Phil. 2:5-7).

Who is this servant we are called to imitate? Only when we remember that he is God Incarnate, true God and true man, do we begin to understand his call to servanthood. As true God, Jesus Christ knows how humanity should live. As true man—the only perfect person who ever lived in human history—Jesus Christ points the path to genuine fulfillment and lasting joy. "To be fully human is to be Christlike, for Jesus was fully human even as he was fully God."[7]

Jesus' kind of servanthood is the way to reach the fullness of human life intended by the Creator for all persons. E. Stanley Jones was right: "The most miserable people in the world are the people who are self-centered, who don't do anything for anybody, except themselves. They are centers of misery with no exception. . . . On the contrary, the happiest people are the people who deliberately take on themselves the sorrows and troubles of others. Their hearts sing with a strange wild joy."[8]

If Jesus is true man, then servanthood is the way to lasting joy.

The path to joy, however, winds through self-denial. No one, perhaps, has put it better than C. S. Lewis:

> Give up your self, and you will find your real self. Lose your life and you will save it. Submit to death, death of your ambitions and favorite wishes every day and death of your whole body in the end: submit with every fibre of your being and you will find eternal life. Keep back nothing. Nothing that you have not given away will ever really be yours. Nothing in you that has not died will ever be raised from the dead. Look for yourself, and you will find in the long run only hatred, loneliness, despair, rage, ruin, and decay. But look for Christ and you will find Him, and with Him everything else thrown in.[9]

To be sure, it is possible to confuse biblical servanthood with a groveling self-denial grounded in self-hatred or an inadequate sense of self-worth. Sometimes women, victims of sexual abuse, and oppressed minorities have been so degraded by others that they lack almost all sense of dignity and worth. Such people think of themselves *less* highly than God does. That is not Christian humility and servanthood. It is self-hatred grounded in sinful abuse. Jesus' kind of servanthood flows from a powerful awareness of our dignity and worth based in the knowledge that the Creator of the universe made us in the divine image and redeemed us at the cross.

What would happen if the church today recovered Jesus' pattern of humble service? If the church truly believed Jesus' word that all who want to be disciples must imitate his servanthood? If significant numbers of Christians dared to become genuine followers of the Servant King? The answer is clear: The world would stop to watch—and be changed.

Dream with me for a bit about how Christian servanthood would transform our evangelism, our call for ethical standards, our plea to heal the family, our call to end abortion, even our political engagement.

Think of the contrast between two kinds of evangelism: evangelism done by conquerors and evangelism done by servants.

Too often, since the time of Constantine, Christians have tried to share the gospel as military conquerors rather than servants. When the Emperor Constantine became a Christian in the early fourth century, he baptized all his troops. That is power evangelism. But it is the power of the sword, not the Spirit. Since then, Christians have dared to tell Muslims that Jesus was the only way to salvation even while they launched vicious crusades and slaughtered hundreds of thousands of Muslims. Christians invited Jews to accept their Messiah as they tolerated anti-Semitic discrimination, pogroms, and the Nazi holocaust.

British missionaries flooded into China right after the British government fought the Opium War with China to force the Chinese to allow Britain to sell opium in China! Hudson Taylor lamented the fact that the opium forced on the Chinese was everywhere in China: "It does more harm in a week than all our missionaries are doing good in a year." When a missionary mentioned hell, one respected man in the audience replied: "Since you foreigners came, China has become hell."[10]

North American Christians sent missionaries to the Indians while their governments broke hundreds of treaties and almost wiped out the native people. Spanish missionaries preached Christ to the indigenous people of South America while their relatives brutally conquered and massacred them. Some Europeans even dared to tell Africans about Christianity while they forced them into slavery. According to some reports, there was even a slave ship that worked out of Charleston called "The Good Ship Jesus."

The difference between that kind of evangelism and servant evangelism patterned after Jesus struck me recently while I was in Malaysia. One Sunday morning I was swept up in praise to the risen Lord as I stood and sang passionately in a charismatic Chinese worship service. I do not remember the song. But suddenly it hit me that I stood in the middle of the largely non-Christian continent of Asia in the predominantly Muslim country of Malaysia, singing that Jesus is Lord of all the earth, the only way to salvation for all people everywhere. The audacity of the claim overwhelmed me.

Slowly I began to reflect on evangelism as servanthood. The evangelism of marauding medieval crusaders or conquering colonial armies has no integrity. But servant evangelists who humbly, sacrificially minister to all the needs of people of other faiths do have integrity when they also invite them to accept the only Savior of the world. Thank God that there were Spanish missionaries who protested, even at great danger and sacrifice, against the slaughter of the Latin American Indians. Thank God there were evangelical students of evangelist Charles Finney who denounced the U.S. government's broken treaties with the Indians as they gently invited those same Native Americans to accept their Lord.

In chapter 9, we saw how Vinay and Colleen Samuel moved from the chair to the floor. Most of the people they serve in the great land of India are Hindus and Muslims. Gently, humbly, they sit on the floor of their little huts to listen to their pain. Together they design programs to battle hunger and disease and increase education and jobs. Through it all they share Christ and invite everyone to accept him.

I've also described Wayne Gordon's radical promise to do anything God asked him to do. It took him to the inner city and ten break-ins at his apartment–the first one the night he and his wife, Anne, returned from their honeymoon–but like Jesus, Wayne and Anne defied danger to serve the poor. The result is powerful evangelism, a rapidly growing church, and scores of transformed inner-city kids.

Servant evangelism is the only kind that is faithful to Jesus. It also works better. In a recent national survey, the Barna Research Group asked the question: "What would make the church more attractive?" The second most common answer was: a church helping the poor and needy.[11]

Servanthood is also essential if we want to reverse the galloping ethical relativism of our time. Few things are more important. Our civilization will collapse if we cannot curb promiscuity, rampant divorce, greed, and the pervasive dishonesty that is corrupting law, business, medicine, and public life. The modern notion that ethical norms are relative personal preferences or cultural biases is rapidly destroying our society. We must return to the long-standing Christian tradition that ethical principles are universally binding. Why? Because they are grounded in the very nature of reality. Christians must issue a ringing call first to the church and then to the larger society to turn away from destructive, individualistic relativism and return to the ethical standards implanted by the Creator and revealed in Scripture.

How we make this appeal, however, is crucial. Some Christian moral crusades–even when they are right in what they uphold–are so harsh, legalistic, and unloving that they cannot be heard. If our actions make homosexuals think we hate them, they will never hear our ethical arguments against homosexual practice. If our attitudes prompt divorcées to feel rejected, they will never hear our claim that lifelong marriage is the way to joy. If young women contemplating abortion experience pro-life Christians as angry demonstrators denouncing them as murderers, they will never hear our plea to respect the life within them.

Servanthood is the key. The gay community in Grand Rapids listens respectfully to Ed Dobson's loving insistence that homosexual practice is sin because they know he loves them and serves them even in death. It is the pastor who gently, patiently, sacrificially walks the painful road month after month with the husband and wife contemplating divorce that can be heard when she pleads with them not to give up on their marriage. It is the Christian families that welcome separated spouses into their homes and promise to be there for them for as long as it takes who can teach Jesus' standard of lifelong marriage covenant with integrity. It is the congregation that embraces rather than ostracizes pregnant, unmarried teenagers that can help society see that sex before marriage and abortion on demand are lousy substitutes for God's way of sexual purity and respect for life.

We should desperately urge society to turn away from its ethical insanity. We should desperately urge Christians boldly to proclaim God's revealed moral standards. But we will never be heard unless we learn how to become servants. We must plead with our broken neighbors like weeping prophets, not denounce them like angry moralists. We must gently throw our arms around all those trapped in sin, love them into the kingdom, and travel with them no matter what the cost in their journey toward wholeness in Christ. Society will change if the first thought that comes to mind when pro-choice advocates, AIDS victims, and practicing homosexuals think of Christians is: "We know they love us because they serve us in our need." Servanthood must be the hallmark of the Christian.

The same is true for the new initiatives urging the restoration of fatherhood in our society. If the family is to survive, men must repent of their ghastly irresponsibility and sinful abandonment of wives and children. Men must again become faithful husbands and responsible fathers. Servanthood, however, is essential. It will not heal our broken families if men come back home with the message: "Move over, baby, the boss is back." Domineering patriarchy is no solution. What we need is the radical servanthood commanded by the apostle Paul. Christian husbands who love and serve their wives in the costly, self-giving way Christ loved the church will make an invaluable contribution to restoring the family and healing the society.

Servanthood is relevant everywhere–even when we think of the environment. Too often Christians have twisted the biblical doctrine of dominion and misunderstood it as domination. Humans *are* created in the image of God and carrots are not. God has given us a special stewardship over the earth. But the biblical text explicitly defines this stewardship in terms of servanthood. As we saw in chapter 10, God commands us "to work *[abad]* and take care of" God's earth (Gen. 2:15). The Hebrew word *abad* actually means serve. The related noun is translated as "slave" or "servant."

Imagine what would happen if even a quarter of the Christians in the world got serious about God's command to serve the creation. Imagine the impact on secular environmentalists if their first thought about Christians was: "They are servants of the earth because they worship the Creator." The result would not be the worship of trees or a preference for plants over persons. Rather, it would be a new movement that honors the Creator by nurturing a gorgeous sustainable creation for our grandchildren and their grandchildren. Biblical environmentalists are servants of creation because they obey the Creator.

Servanthood is even relevant for Christian political activity. Christian politicians who demonize opponents, indulge in half-truths, and angrily attack those who disagree are not obeying Jesus. Their behavior is also counterproductive. Christian politicians who appear primarily interested in gaining power for and protecting the self-interest of Christians are unbiblical. Their actions are also self-defeating.

Politicians who truly understand Jesus will be known first of all as servants. Servants of the weak, servants of their constituents, and even servants of their political opponents. Genuinely Christian politicians will be known as voices for the poor, the weak, and the marginalized. Truly Christian political engagement will persistently remind the nation that God judges societies by what they do to the poorest.

Christian politicians will never forget Jesus' sarcastic condemnation of self-serving rulers who pretend to be helping their people: "The kings of the Gentiles lord it over them; and those who exercise authority over them call themselves Benefactors. But you are not to be like that" (Luke 22:25–26). Instead, Jesus wants leaders who serve their people. "The greatest among you should be like the youngest, and the one who rules like the one who serves. . . . I am among you as one who serves" (Luke 22:26–27). Obviously the first application of these words is to leadership in the church. But surely they also apply to the way a Christian politician should carefully serve the genuine interests of the people.

Politicians who claim to follow the Servant who was also the Truth will serve society as courageous voices for truth. They will refuse to twist the facts even when honesty is costly. They will be fair with opponents. They will serve their nation by promoting honest, serious debate rather than by joining the trend toward distorted half-truths, divisive attack commercials, and character assassination. They will be the last people to repeat unsubstantiated charges and malicious rumors.

Genuine democracy can flourish only with honest debate and a careful search for truth. Justice can grow only if there are strong voices for the poor and weak. Christian politicians who understand their calling as servanthood will play a crucial role in shaping a better future.

Christianity as servanthood could transform our homes and our nations. But that will never happen unless the church's leaders truly become servants.

Surely one of the most astonishing spectacles in all of the Bible is Jesus' disciples quarreling at the Last Supper (Luke 22:24ff.). Jesus had lived for three years among them as a servant. He had taught and modeled humble service.

Moments before, he had just given the apostles the bread and the wine as the eternal memorial of his ultimate act of self-giving at Calvary. It is at this incredible moment that the disciples argue angrily about which of them is the greatest! Jesus must have been near despair.

I fear that he still is. As Christ looks on the contemporary church, he sees church leaders who abuse power, live extravagantly, and jockey for fame and prestige. He must weep.

Thank God that is not the total picture. There are scores of unknown servant leaders scattered through the church. There are also shining examples of prominent humble leaders. Mother Teresa led powerfully with her costly service to the poor, the weak, the unborn, and the marginalized. Decade after decade, Billy Graham continues to model integrity and humility in spite of his fame and influence. When you meet him you sense the spirit of a servant.

Pastor by pastor, deacon by deacon, we must return to Jesus' teaching on servant leadership. As that happens, our congregations will grow in numbers, integrity, and impact in the world.

Jesus' gospel is what our broken world needs. Biblical ethical standards are what our crazy society longs for, even without knowing it. But they will never be able to hear our message unless we share it as servants.

As I prepared to write this chapter, I reread Bill Hybels's marvelous book *Descending into Greatness.* It is a powerful plea for Christian servanthood. The more I read, the more I felt I had barely begun to understand the Servant at the core of Christian faith. But I want to know him better and follow in his steps more faithfully. I'm convinced that means embracing servanthood in ever deeper ways as central to everything I do. The more faithfully Christians today follow the Servant King, the more our evangelism will have power, our marriages will have wholeness, and our societies will enjoy justice.

Epilogue

Only God knows what the archangel Gabriel will see as he watches the twenty-first century unfold. But you and I can dream and pray—and work.

I dream of a new century that will leave even Gabriel dumbfounded with joy. I picture Gabriel marveling in astonishment as more and more Christians surrender unconditionally to the risen Lord and open their total being to the fullness of the Spirit. They live like Jesus. They care for the whole person. God raises up more and more Wayne Gordons who look daily into the face of the Lord and promise: "I'll do anything you want me to do with my life." By the millions, broken prostitutes like Lola, twisted drug dealers like Juan de Jesús, and self-centered middle-class professionals are radically, beautifully transformed.

On every continent, growing congregations of faithful believers flourish. In every country, city, and village, Jesus' devout followers eagerly invite others to accept the Lord they adore, and then they patiently walk with these new Christians, offering God's tough love that transforms mangled lives into wholeness, beauty, and joy.

For the first time in history, vast numbers of Asians embrace Christ. China slowly becomes more free and just as a huge minority of its billion and a quarter people become disciples of Christ. Africa becomes not only the continent with the highest percentage of Christians, but also the place where biblical discipleship is lived out most fully. Revival sweeps across North and South America, renewing tired, lukewarm churches. Faithful Christians provide the morality and integrity that slowly blesses Russia with freedom and justice. Even Western Europe—which Gabriel once watched in horror as Christianity almost collapsed in the twentieth century—enjoys a powerful resurgence of biblical faith.

As Gabriel watches with joy and amazement, he realizes that no magic formula has appeared. The marvelous growth is not due to some new management idea or technological breakthrough. Everywhere genuine Christians struggle hard. Again and again they fail. But temporary setbacks cannot stop them.

As Gabriel examines this global explosion of Christian faith, the secret becomes crystal clear. Actually, it is no secret at all. It is just that somehow, in God's grace, tens of millions of contemporary Christians truly believe the old, old story: They love Jesus with all their heart, mind, and strength; they surrender every fiber of their being to him; and they imitate Christ's love for the whole person. No matter what the cost, they give themselves and their resources to empower the poor, bind up the battered, and bring hope to the despairing. Constantly, eagerly, passionately, they share their best treasure, Jesus the Savior, inviting others to embrace his forgiveness and healing. And they teach the new believers what they wholeheartedly seek for themselves—to let their glorious God and Savior become the unconditional Lord of every corner of life.

The result is stunning. In spite of tragic imperfection, tens of thousands of congregations actually resemble what Gabriel knows heaven is like. In spite of painful failure, tens of millions of Christian marriages overflow with contagious joy and integrity. In spite of wrenching injustice, whole societies become more free, fair, and whole. And tens of millions, each year, discover for the first time the incredible joy of personal faith in the Savior.

Gabriel is astonished at the resulting beauty and goodness. But even more he marvels at the simplicity of the original plan. All it takes to spread the gospel, renew the family, and reform society is a small band of genuine Christians as dedicated to Christ as the first 120.

As Gabriel watches their impact, he is astonished to realize that the genuine Christians are still just a minority of those who claim the name. That minority, however, has an awesome power. And the reason is so simple.

Day by day, they look into the face of Jesus Christ and whisper quietly: "Lord there is nothing I want as much as to be more like you. If you give me the power, I'll do whatever you want me to do with my life."

NOTES

Introduction

1. David B. Barrett and Todd M. Johnson, *Our Globe and How to Reach It* (Birmingham: New Hope, 1990), 32.

2. See *Hunger 1995: Causes of Hunger* (Silver Spring: Bread for the World Institute, 1994), 10.

3. I omit any discussion of what could be the most devastating threat to Christian faith—namely the pervasive secularism that comes with modernity. For an introduction, see the articles by Os Guinness and others in the October/December 1993 issue of *Transformation*.

4. George Barna (1994 data) quoted in Charles Colson, "The Year of the Neopagan," *Christianity Today* (March 6, 1995), 88.

5. See National Institute of Justice, *Research in Brief* (February 1994); Janet Karsten Larson, "Society Behind Bars," *Christian Century* (November 10, 1993), 1123.

6. See chapter 8 of my book *Cup of Water, Bread of Life: Inspiring Stories about Overcoming Lopsided Christianity* (Grand Rapids: Zondervan, 1994). Wayne Gordon also tells his story in the book *Real Hope in Chicago* (Grand Rapids: Zondervan, 1995).

7. I do not mean to argue that God only works through Christians. As Lord of history, God can use all people for his purposes. But God has chosen the church as his special instrument of salvation and transformation.

Chapter 1: Searing Holiness, Forgiving Love

1. Tammy Bakker and Cliff Duddley, *I Gotta Be Me* (Green Forest, Ark.: New Leaf Press, 1978).

2. For a more extensive discussion see chapter 5 (and also 3, 4, and 6) of my *One-Sided Christianity?* (Grand Rapids: Zondervan, 1993); 2d ed., *Good News and Good Works* (Grand Rapids: Baker, 1999).

3. That is not to say that all will be saved. I reject universalism (see my *One-Sided Christianity?* 128–31).

4. Jerry Bridges, *The Practice of Godliness* (Colorado Springs: NavPress, 1983), 264.

Chapter 2: Conformed to Christ

1. Robert Ellsberg, ed., *Gandhi on Christianity* (Maryknoll: Orbis, 1991), 32.

2. See my *One-Sided Christianity?* chapters 3 and 4.

3. These and other stories are told in much more detail in my *Cup of Water, Bread of Life.*

Chapter 3: Renewing Marriage and Family

1. Originally published as "Uncle Jesse" in *Moody Monthly,* June 1989, 71–73, this story has been reprinted in more places than anything else I have written.

2. Three quarters of all U.S. spouses are sexually unfaithful. Rodney Clapp, *Families at the Crossroads* (Downers Grove, Ill.: InterVarsity, 1993), 117. Amy E. Black, *For the Sake of the Children: Reconstructing American Divorce Policy,* Crossroads Monographs, no. 2 (Philadelphia: Evangelicals for Social Action, 1995), 12.

3. Barbara Dafoe Whitehead, "Dan Quayle Was Right," *Atlantic Monthly* (April 1993), 47.

4. This is my memory of the words and may not be an exact quotation.

5. Fortunately, the evidence suggests that committed Christians (measured by frequency of church attendance and praying together as couples) get divorced less frequently; see Paul and Richard Meier, *Family Foundations* (Grand Rapids: Baker, 1981). Unfortunately, their data is not recent nor is it based on extensive studies.

6. This is not an exact citation.

Chapter 4: Immersed in Prayer, Filled with the Spirit

1. Richard Lovelace, *Dynamics of Spiritual Life: An Evangelical Theology of Renewal* (Downers Grove, Ill.: InterVarsity Press, 1979), 381–82.

2. Elton Trueblood, *The New Man for Our Time* (New York: Harper and Row, 1970), 66–67.

3. Lovelace, *Dynamics,* 392.

4. Andrew Murray, *With Christ in the School of Prayer* (Old Tappan, N.J.: Revell, 1953), 102–3.

5. Ibid., 8.

6. See for example, David Bryant, *The Hope at Hand: National and World Revival for the Twenty-First Century* (Grand Rapids: Baker, 1995).

7. Richard Foster, *Celebration of Discipline* (San Francisco: HarperSanFrancisco, 1988), 135.

8. See Carolyn Boyd, *The Apostle of Hope: The Dr. Kriengsak Story* (West Sussex: Sovereign World, 1991).

9. David Barret, "Annual Statistical Table on Global Mission," *International Bulletin of Missionary Research* (January 1995), 25.

10. Charles Kraft, *Christianity with Power* (Ann Arbor: Servant Publications, 1989).

Chapter 5: A Little Picture of Heaven

1. See chapter 4 of my *Rich Christians in an Age of Hunger* (Dallas: Word, 1997).

2. Quoted in *Rich Christians*, 82.

3. For a much longer discussion, see my *One-Sided Christianity?* chapters 3–4.

4. *Hunger 1995: Causes of Hunger* (Silver Spring: Bread for the World Institute, 1994), 50–51.

5. *The Works of John Wesley,* 14 vols. (Grand Rapids: Zondervan, n.d. [reprint of 1872 edition]), vol. 8, 253–54.

6. "The Memphis Miracle," *Ministries Today* (January–February 1995), 36–42, 66.

Chapter 6: Loving Both Body and Soul

1. For more detail about the Franklins and Rock/Circle, see chapter 4 of *Cup of Water, Bread of Life.*

2. John Stott, *Christian Mission in the Modern World* (Downers Grove, Ill.: InterVarsity Press, 1975), 30.

3. John Perkins, *A Call to Wholistic Ministry* (St. Louis: Open Door Press, 1980), 43–44.

4. Quoted in *One-Sided Christianity?* 175.

5. *Redemptoris Missio,* 83.

6. I want to thank Dr. Mike Moore and Dr. Carolyn Klaus for the information about Juan de Jesús.

Chapter 7: Must We Knock Down Other People's Candles?

1. *The Best of A. W. Tozer: 52 Favorite Chapters,* compiled by Warren W. Wiersbe (Grand Rapids: Baker, 1978), 72.

2. See the discussion and further references in John M. Frame, *Evangelical Reunion: Denominations and the Body of Christ* (Grand Rapids: Baker, 1991), 26.

3. Ibid., 28.

4. See Frame's helpful discussion of toleration for some doctrinal differences in chapter 8 of his *Evangelical Reunion.*

5. Nicholas Lossky, et al., eds., *Dictionary of the Ecumenical Movement* (Geneva: WCC Publications, 1991), 1097.

6. For more information, write the Evangelical Environmental Network, 10 East Lancaster Avenue, Wynnewood, PA 19096.

7. "Evangelicals and Catholics Together," reprinted in *First Things* (May 1994), 15–22. Unfortunately the document lacks the prophets' and Jesus' ringing call to seek justice for the poor.

8. Frame, *Evangelical Reunion,* 167.

Chapter 8: Bedroom, Boardroom, and Ballot Box

1. Garth Lean, *God's Politician* (Colorado Springs: Helmers & Howard, 1987), 38.

2. Exact figures are unavailable. From 1780–1860, about 4.5 million slaves were forcibly brought to the Americas. See David Eltis, *Economic Growth and the Ending of the Transatlantic Slave Trade* (London: Oxford, 1987), 249.

3. Ernest Marshall Howse, *Saints in Politics: The "Clapham Sect" and the Growth of Freedom* (Toronto: University of Toronto Press, 1952), 28.

4. For a good introduction to the secularization that has accompanied modernity, see the articles and bibliography in *Transformation* (October–December 1993), especially the article by Os Guinness.

5. See the declaration and commentary in Vinay Samuel, Herb Schlossberg, and Ronald J. Sider, eds., *Christianity and Economics in the Post-Cold War Era: The Oxford Declaration and Beyond* (Grand Rapids: Eerdmans, 1994). This conference brought together biblical principles and careful economic analysis producing what I call in this chapter an *examined* ideology.

6. Christopher Wright calls this summary of biblical principles a paradigm; see "The Use of the Bible in Social Ethics," *Transformation* (January–March 1984), 10.

7. Evangelicals for Social Action's Crossroads program produces careful scholarly analysis and popular updates on current issues in public policy. Also available from ESA is Ronald J. Sider, *Politics and the Bible: A Study Guide for Christians.* Write ESA, 10 Lancaster Avenue, Wynnewood, PA 19096, or call 1-800-650-6600.

8. For a careful evaluation of today's market economies, see the fourth edition of my *Rich Christians in an Age of Hunger* (Dallas: Word, 1997), 139–47, 232–43.

9. See my "Toward a Biblical Perspective on Equality," *Interpretation* (April 1989), 156–69.

10. See Donald W. Dayton, *Discovering an Evangelical Heritage* (New York: Harper and Row, 1976), chapters 2, 4, 8.

11. Ibid., 69.

12. See the marvelous story of how Michael Cardone has done that in his *Never Too Late for a New Beginning* (Grand Rapids: Revell, 1988).

Chapter 9: Moving from the Chair to the Floor

1. For a much longer account, see chapter 3 of my *Cup of Water, Bread of Life.*

2. See *Hunger 1995: Causes of Hunger,* Fifth Annual Report on the State of World Hunger (Silver Spring: Bread for the World Institute, 1994), 2.

3. For references for these statistics, see my *One-Sided Christianity?* 191–92.

4. *Hunger 1995,* 50–51; see also Greg Thompson, "The Rich, the Poor and the Earth," *Together* (January–March 1995), 1–3.

5. It may be, as some exegetes suggest, that the first reference, both here and in Matthew 25, is to brothers and sisters who confess Christ. But Jesus clearly teaches that anyone in need is our neighbor (Matt. 5:43–45; Luke 10:29–37). See further, *Rich Christians,* 58–59.

6. Ronald J. Sider, *For They Shall Be Fed: Scripture Readings and Prayers for a Just World* (Dallas: Word, 1997).

7. See John and Sylvia Ronsvalle, *The State of Church Giving through 1992* (Champaign: Empty Tomb Press, 1995).

8. I have tried to develop a biblical understanding of equality and equity in my "Toward a Biblical Perspective on Equality," *Interpretation* (April 1989), 156–69.

9. For much more detail on David Bussau and the Bali church, see chapters 6 and 7 of *Cup of Water, Bread of Life.*

10. David B. Barrett, "Annual Statistical Table," *International Bulletin of Missionary Research* (January 1995), 25.

11. For a copy of the Agra Covenant on Christian Capital, write to Agra Covenant, 10 East Lancaster Avenue, Wynnewood, PA 19096-3495 (Fax 610-649-8090).

Chapter 10: Tending the Garden without Worshiping It

1. To receive a free copy, write to EEN, 10 Lancaster Avenue, Wynnewood, PA 19096, or call 610-645-9392.

2. Billy Graham, *Approaching Hoofbeats* (Waco: Word, 1983), 195.

3. Ibid., 196.

4. Some good recent books: Lester Brown, *State of the World, 1995* (New York and London: W. W. Norton, 1995); Bob Hall and Mary Lee Kerr, *1993–1994 Green Index: A State-by-State Guide to the Nation's Environmental Health* (Washington, D.C.: Island Press, 1994); Geoffrey Lean and Don Hinrichsen, *Atlas of the Environment,* 2d ed. (New York: HarperCollins, 1994); National Academy of Sciences, *One Earth, One Future: Our Changing Global Environment* (Washington, D.C.: National Academy Press, 1992); Union of Concerned Scientists, *World Scientists' Briefing Book* (26 Church Street, Cambridge, MA 02238, 1993).

5. Available from the Union of Concerned Scientists, 26 Church Street, Cambridge, MA 02238.

6. Lester R. Brown, et al., *State of the World 1995* (New York: Norton, 1995), 5.

7. Ibid., 6.

8. William Stevens, "Scientists Confront Renewed Backlash on Global Warming," *New York Times* (September 14, 1993), B-5.

9. "World Scientists' Warning to Humanity."

10. Calvin B. De Witt, *Earth-Wise: A Biblical Response to Environmental Issues* (Grand Rapids: CRC Publications, 1994), 30–31.

11. Ibid., 30.

12. "World Scientists' Warning to Humanity."

13. Ghillean Prance, "A Wealth of Species," in Jonathan Porritt, *Save the Earth* (Toronto: MacClelland and Stewart, 1991), 75–79.

14. Lynn White, "The Historical Roots of Our Ecological Crisis," *Science* 155, no. 3767 (March 1967), 1203–7.

15. For a variety of helpful materials, contact EEN, 10 Lancaster Avenue, Wynnewood, PA 19096 (1-800-650-6600; www.esa-online.org/een/).

Conclusion: Christian Faith as Servanthood

1. See chapter 6 of Ed Dobson's book *Simplicity: Reconciling Your Life with Your Values* (Grand Rapids: Zondervan, 1995).

2. Ibid.

3. James Davison Hunter, "The Williamsburg Charter Survey," *The Journal of Law and Religion* (1990), 268.

4. *New York Times* (August 29, 1993). It is astounding that the *Times* would publish such absurdity.

5. Timothy B. Shah, *National Service: Will AmeriCorps Serve America?* "Crossroads Monograph Series in Faith and Public Policy," vol.1, no. 1 (1995), 29–30. This new monograph series is available from Evangelicals for Social Action, 10 Lancaster Avenue, Wynnewood, PA 19096; 1-800-650-6600.

6. See Jeremias's discussion of the views of Jesus and the early church in W. Zimmerli and J. Jeremias, *The Servant of God,* Studies in Biblical Theology, no. 20 (Naperville: Alec R. Allenson, 1957), 88ff., 99ff.

7. Shah, *National Service,* 30.

8. E. Stanley Jones, *The Unshakable Kingdom* (Nashville: Abingdon, 1972), 54.

9. C. S. Lewis, *Mere Christianity* (New York: Macmillan, 1986), 180.

10. Quoted from *Encyclopedia of Missions* (New York: Funk and Wagnalls, 1904), 153.

11. *Never on a Sunday: The Challenge of the Unchurched* (Glendale, Cal.: The Barna Research Group, 1990), 24.

Ronald J. Sider (Ph.D., Yale University), professor of theology and culture at Eastern Baptist Theological Seminary in Philadelphia, is president of Evangelicals for Social Action and publisher for *Prism* and *Creation Care* magazines. He is the author of over twenty books, including the best-selling *Rich Christians in an Age of Hunger*.

EVANGELICALS FOR SOCIAL ACTION

ESA is a national association of Christians dedicated to "Living like Jesus"—living out a genuine faith in our lives and communities.

Jesus is Lord of our whole lives, and our lives must be subject to the whole of his gospel. ESA provides a network and resource for Christians committed to this kind of "holistic" discipleship and ministry in our lost and hurting world. Together we can share the good news of Jesus Christ through word and deed.

Join ESA and become a part of an exciting movement including . . .

PRISM> ESA's bimonthly magazine will equip, empower, inform, and inspire you to live more like Jesus, growing a genuine faith in every part of your life. PRISM offers insightful, biblical reflection on the world in which we live—stories and strategies for effective outreach and ministry.

Christian Citizenship> ESA helps Christians to be active, engaged, and responsible citizens. PRISM features a regular "Washington Update," providing a biblical perspective on the latest political developments in our nation's capital. Our Crossroads program brings together Christian scholars for a deeper look at important issues of public policy.

Caring for Creation> ESA hosts the Evangelical Environmental Network (EEN), a network of Christian organizations making care for creation an integral part of their work. World Vision, Habitat for Humanity, and InterVarsity Christian Fellowship are among the members of this environmental network. ESA also produces *Creation Care* magazine, a biblical, environmental quarterly.

Ministry Networks> Becoming a member of ESA makes you a part of a dynamic network of Christians throughout America. Network 9:35 is our exciting new network of churches and pastors committed to the genuine faith and holistic ministry described in Matthew 9:35. ESA's Generous Christians Campaign is a rapidly growing movement of individuals giving sacrificially of their time and resources to help share Jesus' love with the poor, the hungry, and the outcast.

Join Us!

Evangelicals for Social Action • 10 Lancaster Avenue • Wynnewood, PA 19096
1-800-650-6600 • esa@esa-online.org